THE SILVER LINK LIBRARY OF RAILWAY MODELLING

●

MODEL RAILWAYS EXPLAINED

BEYOND THE BEGINNING

The author's former model railway, West Haven.

THE SILVER LINK LIBRARY OF RAILWAY MODELLING

•

MODEL RAILWAYS EXPLAINED
BEYOND THE BEGINNING

The onward development of
The Newcomer's Guide to Model Railways
Brian Lambert

© Brian Lambert 2021

All rights reserved. No part of this publication may be reproduced, stored in a retrieval system or transmitted, in any form or by any means, electronic, mechanical, photocopying, recording or otherwise, without prior permission in writing from Silver Link Books, Mortons Media Group Ltd.

First published in 2021

British Library Cataloguing in Publication Data

A catalogue record for this book is available from the British Library.

ISBN 978 1 85794 545 4

Silver Link Books
Mortons Media Group Limited
Media Centre
Morton Way
Horncastle
LN9 6JR
Tel/Fax: 01507 529535

email: sohara@mortons.co.uk
Website: www.nostalgiacollection.com

Printed and bound in the Czech Republic

Publisher's note: The electrical details and procedures described in this book are to the best of the author's knowledge and belief both accurate and safe. However great care must always be taken when assembling and using electrical equipment, and neither the publisher nor the author can accept responsibility for any accidents or loss that may occur. If in doubt, always consult a qualified electrician.

Acknowledgements

I have to thank all those who have provided me with assistance for this book or allowed me to photograph items they manufacturer or sell. Without their help and support such a publication would not have been possible. In particular these are Gaugemaster Controls Ltd, DCC Concepts Ltd, and Train-Tech, together with a myriad of modellers and railway enthusiasts whose images have been freely given.

Recommended websites:
www.brian-lambert.co.uk (my own website)
www.ModelRailwayForum.co..uk (general model railway forum)
www.NewRailwayModellers.co.uk (general model railway forum)
www.MERG.co.uk (model railway electronics)
www.hebeiltd.com.cn/calculator/v5/led.php (LED resistor calculator)
www.ukmodelshops.co.uk (general model shop, UK clubs and exhibition details)
www.2mm.org.uk/articles/cv29 calculator.htm (DCC CV29 calculator)
www.2mm.org.uk (2mm scale association)
www.ngaugesociety.com (N Gauge Society)
www.doubleogauge.com (OO Gauge Association)
www.mortons.co.uk. (publisher of Silver Link and other transport books and magazines)

Contents

Introduction 6

1 The beginnings 7
2 Baseboards 10
3 Track 13
4 Wiring 18
5 Train control 22
6 Construction kits 28
7 Point control 33
8 Digital Command Control (DCC) 38
9 Special scenic effects 55
10 Basic electronics 62
11 Lineside detailing 75
12 Railway signalling 82
13 Electrification – third rail and OLE 89
14 The '365' layout 99

Index 131

Introduction

My hobby has been model railways for many years, since I was given a Tri-ang Princess Elizabeth train set as a then eight-year-old schoolboy for Christmas. Over the years I have gained much modelling knowledge from practical experience and belonging to model railway clubs, not to mention the wealth of knowledge gained from working on the 'real thing' from a young post-school teenager through to my retirement.

My website – www.brian-lambert.co.uk – has helped many modellers with technical problems and given myself huge enjoyment in compiling it.

My first published book, *The Newcomer's Guide to Model Railways*, published in 2009 (ISBN 98-1-85794-329-0) has, according to my publisher Silver Link, sold well and given many readers a great helping hand in their hobby. So, it was deemed necessary that I should produce a second book that would enhance the first, but would try mainly not to cover the same ground too much. While in these pages I write about generic items and often reference the real thing, there are many regional variations, and these cannot be taken into account within the confines of this book. I would recommend that before starting any regional- or era-based project, undertake a good deal of research to gain the correct facts. Internet searches, books and perhaps visits to preserved railways or to the real places will usually reveal plenty of detail.

If you are starting out in the hobby or returning to it after several years of absence and have not obtained a copy of *The Newcomer's Guide to Model Railways*, I suggest it might be an advantage to obtain a copy and enjoy the contents.

I would like to take the opportunity to thank those who have given their permission to use images from commercial sources and the retailers who have helped with some of the aspects of this second book. Also thanks must go to my wife Sue, who has seen railways built in her conservatory and half of a double garage and never complains about the mess or part-finished work that often lays scattered about when I'm making railway items. Bless you, Sue, for your patience. Also thanks to our friend Elaine for her proofreading of the text, even if she didn't quite understand much of its meaning!

I hope you enjoy the items you are about to read and hopefully they will help and possibly nudge you into producing a great model railway layout.

All content is given in good faith. E&OE.

1
The beginnings

Beginning in model railway construction can be a daunting initial experience for the newcomer looking in a hobby shop's window or using the internet, and for those who have already obtained a train set and wish to progress further. Jargon is often used and some terminology has never been heard before! Electrical wiring petrifies many, while carrying out scenic work appears more to belong to an artist or sculptor rather than a railway modeller! But fear not – by taking each issue in their basic sequential part of construction, this book should lead the modeller from novice to experienced layout builder in a fairly brief time.

The aim of the chapters within this book is to guide and help the progression from a train set to a fully operational model railway. I mention the real thing at times as this is, of course, where our modelling is derived.

I will cover track-laying, scenery, electrical work and digital control, and much more. But before we progress further, the modeller needs to understand some of the terminology and jargon used.

AC Alternating Current in the UK is at 50Hz, but 60Hz in some other countries including North America. AC swaps polarity around the zero-voltage point at the rate shown by the Hertz value.

Ballast The stones used to retain the track in place.

Cess The area between the outer ballast shoulder and the often unkempt ground or other railway boundary such as a fence or wall.

Chair The metal plate fixed on top of the sleeper on which the rail sits. The rail is retained in place in the chair by keys (see below).

Check rail A secondary inner rail used to guide the wheel flanges at a set of points, preventing the wheel from riding up and ensuring that the wheels take the correct course or route.

Closure rails The fixed non-moving rails immediately after the switch rails and immediately before the points frog (see below).

DC Direct Current. The output from all batteries, and can also be from rectified AC. It is a single directional flow of current as it maintains the positive above the zero voltage.

DCC Digital Command Control. This is a means of controlling and operating a model railway by digital data signals transmitted via the rails to a locomotive that is fitted with a decoder.

Decoder A small electronic circuit board sometimes called a 'chip', which converts digital instructions into operation outputs for electric motor control, lighting, sounds or operating accessories.

Fishplate Also known as a rail joiner, this is a device used to connect two abutting rail ends securely together. It keeps the two rails in line both vertically and horizontally. Normally on the real railway two are used, one on each side of the rail, held to the rail by bolts and nuts; depending on type there are normally four or six bolts per fishplate joint. Due to their construction they allow a small amount of expansion and contraction to occur within the joint. In model railways they are normally a slide-on fit. Their purpose on the model is normally to hold the two abutting rails in register with each other and to provide an electrical path from rail to rail.

Four foot This is real railway terminology for the space between the two running rails, which on standard gauge railways is 4ft 8½in (1,435mm).

Frog This really isn't true terminology and is not used on the real railway! It is actually a fixed crossing, but for some reason model railways have opted to use the term for switches to describe the place where the two rails converge then separate again out to the route required.

Gauge This was covered in some detail in *The Newcomer's Guide To Model Railways*, but basically it is the distance between the two running rails' inner faces. Often gauge is confused with scale (see below), but the two are different.

IRJ Insulated Rail Joiner. This is similar to a fishplate but is normally made from plastic or nylon and separates electrically the abutting rails.

Key The device that retains the rail in place in a chair. The key may be made of sprung steel or, on older track sections, a hardwood block. These are usually driven in place and are a tight fit onto the outside or web of the rail, but they still allow the rail to slide under expansion and contraction in the chair.

Point motor A device that moves the point switch blades from one side to the other. It is often electrically operated, but on the real railway can also be operated by air (pneumatic) or oil (hydraulic).

Point Sometimes called a turnout, this track arrangement changes the direction of a train. Points come in single turnouts to the left or right, Y-shaped, three-way, or single and double slips. Points are made up of various components and terms and it is very handy to know the names of these and their place or use. Points normal is the position of the switch blades that allows the train to pass on the most-used direction or route, often, but not always, in the straight-ahead direction. Points reverse is the opposite of normal, where the switch blades allow the train to pass in the lesser direction or route, often but not always the turn-out direction or route.

Rail This has three basic components: the head or top surface on which the train's wheels travel; the foot, being the bottom part of the rail; and the web, the thinner area that connects the head to the foot. In model form the size of the rail is referenced by the use of the word 'Code' followed by a series of numbers that represent the overall height of the rail in thousandths of an inch, e.g. Code 100 is 100 thousandths of an inch tall.

Rail joiner See Fishplate

Route The direction the train is to take along the track.

Scale The relative measurement between the model and the real-life item. Scales may cause much confusion for the unwary. The main scales found in the model shop are N, HO, OO and O. N normally runs on a track gauge of 9mm, HO and OO share the same track and run on 16.5mm track, while O uses track with a inside edge rail-to-rail measurement of 32mm. Many are confused by HO and OO using the same track, but HO is really the nearer to correct scale and is used by all European and US modellers, while OO is a scale not normally available outside of the UK, and technically the rolling stock is oversized for the track it runs on. Model railways also use many other scales, but the main ones found off the shelf in model shops are 4mm to 1 foot (in the UK this is OO) and 2mm to the foot (N), or described by their ratio, e.g. 1:76.2 (OO), commonly referenced as 1:76, 1:86 (HO), or 1:148 (N in the UK)

Signal 'off' This signal aspect indicates 'proceed'. In the case of a semaphore signal the arm is raised or lowered to approximately 45 degrees from horizontal. Where a colour light signal is used, 'off' is any aspect or aspects displayed that indicate proceed.

Signal 'on' This is the aspect indicating 'danger' or 'stop'. When a stop signal's arm is horizontal it indicates stop, while a distant signal's arm at horizontal indicates 'caution'. For colour light signals, red means stop, while a single yellow at its lowest possible aspect may be passed at caution.

Six foot The gap between two adjacent running lines on the real railway.

Sleeper The support that holds the two running rails apart. On the real railway they can be made of wood, concrete or steel, and some have even been produced in plastic!

Stock rails The two fixed outer rails of a set of points.

Stretcher bar Also known as a tie bar, in the model this is the part of the point that connects the two moving switch rails together. Often it is also the place where a point motor or other point control method is connected, moving the point switch rails over and back as required.

Switch rails The moving rails of a set of points that direct the wheels of the train in the correct direction or route.

Ten foot Another track spacing gap between two adjacent tracks, but wider, and often used on the real railway where four or more lines are running parallel – the ten foot would be in the middle of the four lines.

Tip The single end of a set of points, more explicitly the end of a moving switch rail.

Toe The single line or beginning of the point.

Track This is fairly straightforward, as it is what our trains run along. In model form it is mainly two-rail, and although some three-rail track is still sold, it is becoming rarer with the passing of each year.

Up and down These terms refer to the direction of travel. In the UK this is quite often referenced when travelling towards or away from London, but not always; generally up is towards London, and down is away from the city, but there are many cases where this doesn't apply! Note: in the UK trains travel normally on the left-hand side, the same side as cars on the road. Again, there are some exceptions to the rule, but this is the normal practice.

Wheel flange The raised inner lip on the wheels of all railway locomotives, carriages and wagons, which keep the wheels on the top of the running rail and guides them and train through points and crossings (locomotives don't have steering wheels!).

While the above is far from an exhaustive list, it should help the modeller to become more familiar with model and real railway terminology, although it applies to UK railway practice. Non-UK railways will use similar terms, but may have local terminology for specific items, e.g. turnout for points, ties for sleepers, etc.

2
Baseboards

Firstly, there is a need to decide what the track is to be laid upon. This is the 'baseboard', and is not the dining room table or even worse the floor, where dust and carpet fluff will very quickly cause your new models to develop poor running or even fail stopped. It should be remembered that a baseboard is the foundation of the model railway. It is exactly like the foundations of your home. If it is poorly made, in the end it will lead to anything it supports becoming weakened and will cause poor running due to unlevel track, while any scenic work will crack or break away. So the best advice I can offer is to make the baseboard solid enough to support your own weight (Sumo wrestlers exempt!), without it flexing or buckling!

I have found plywood to be one of the best materials from which to construct a baseboard. If possible use Marine or Birch plywood, 9mm or 12mm thick, supported on a timber frame, as its relatively light in weight but equally quite rigid when well braced. 6mm plywood can be used, but needs additional underside bracing to prevent sagging. Medium Density Fibreboard (MDF) is also used, but has two main disadvantages in that it is very hard to drive track pins into and is prone to soaking up any moisture, so if used it needs all surfaces to be thoroughly sealed. It can be sealed with paint, gloss or matt, varnish or even PVA glue diluted with water, 50/50 or 60/40 water to glue. Ensure that all edges are treated, especially where the layout is in an environment where airborne moisture may be present – garages or sheds are two such examples.

Hardboard (known as Masonite in the US) is not a suitable material as it is too thin and very hard. Chipboard has been used by many modellers, but weight is an important factor. It too needs good bracing underneath and the edges are prone to breaking away if knocked slightly. Plasterboard is totally unsuitable, as is soft board, sometimes known as Insulation board. Some have use solid insulation foam sheets sold by the building trade for insulating wall cavities, etc; the 2-inch (50mm) variety is mainly used. It offers a very light weight and considerable thickness, but its main disadvantage is the thickness – installing point motors below the baseboard is virtually impossible. You will need to mount the motors either to the points' underside by creating a large hole in the foam to accommodate the motor, or use surface motors. It can also be seriously affected by contamination from some solvents.

The use of a soft sheet material known as Sundeala is one that is often recommended by model shops. Sundeala is technically a pin-board material made from recycled paper. It accepts track pins easily and retains them too, but is extremely prone to sagging between supporting timbers. I recommend that if Sundeala is the chosen material it should be laid on top of a more stable and firmer sub-base, such as 6mm plywood or MDF, which will help to prevent any sagging. Sundeala board needs to be conditioned for a few days prior to use and, if used anywhere that is slightly damp, needs to be well sealed on all edges plus top and bottom. Sundeala doesn't cut too well either – a sharp large-sized craft knife or a fine-toothed saw are best. Flush doors have been used, but these tend mainly to be supplied as 6ft 6in (1,981mm) long by widths of between 24 inches (610mm) to 33 inches (838mm). While a modern internal flush hollow door may seem like an ideal baseboard, its physical size makes is not easily moved around indoors, and its thickness can be a problem too. Using internal doors might necessitate joining them together to make one reasonably sized baseboard, then there is the problem of not being able to reach the furthest places from the front or side edges – and these will always be the locations where track cleaning or derailments need to be resolved!

Having chosen the baseboard material, now comes the decision of how to support the boarding. For many years, and still used today, 2in x 1in (44mm x 21mm) Planed Square Edge (PSE) timber has been used. The timber bracing is installed with the narrow edge to the underside of the baseboard. Equally, thinner but deeper timber can be used, such as ¾in x 2¾in (18mm x 69mm) PSE. Two timbers are used, one each along the front and rear edges, and two at each end. Intermediate cross timbers are also fitted and spaced apart inside the outer edge framing. The distance between these internal framing timbers will depend on the baseboard thickness used – thinner boards need more bracing timbers underneath. Typically the bracing is placed at 12-inch (305mm) to 16-inch (406mm) centres. Simple square-cut butt joints will suffice, though more advanced carpentry joints can be used. The simple butt joints can be PVA glued and screwed or nailed together. Screws are always better if possible; drill a pilot hole smaller then the screw's size to help stop the end of the timber splitting. Increase the timber thickness or its depth where longer timber spans are used.

Alternatives to PSE timber framing are plywood or MDF with a thickness of around ½ inch to ¾ inch (12mm to 18mm) and cut to between 3 inches and 4 inches (76mm to 101mm) deep. Plywood makes a very strong framing. Slotted metal angle can be used, as well as metal angle iron, but overall weight is then a problem, as also will be the cost of the material.

Now comes the decision as to how to support our baseboard. What height should the baseboard be is one question frequently asked. Unfortunately there is no hard and fast rule – it is really what suits you or the person who is to operate the layout. A low height might suit children, but can cause severe backache to taller operators, especially during the construction stages. I use a baseboard height of 39 inches (1,000mm) above the floor. Some layout builders prefer to have their baseboards near their eye level, and taller board heights are not uncommon – 4 or more feet is tall!

Straight fixed timber legs can be used, held to the layout with coach bolts, washers and wing nuts on semi-portable layouts, or glued and screwed to the framing on permanent layouts, screwing through the baseboard bracing into the legs. Trestles can be either home-made or purchased as builders' trestles. Drop-down legs that are hinged to the baseboard framing are commonly used on portable layouts, but they all need an additional diagonal brace to hold the leg in the opened position. Whatever method is chosen, it is essential that the support

A typical home-made layout trestle. Note the notches cut in the top cross members to allow secure fitting of the layout's underside bracing timbers. This example sets the layout's baseboard top at 950mm above the floor.

is rigid and can easily take the full weight of the baseboard and possibly the operator leaning on the layout. When using timber, the very minimum for straight legs is 2in x 2in (50mm x 50mm) PSE, but thicker is better. I have successfully used stud walling timber called CLS (Canadian Lumber Standard) timber. I have found 1½in x 2½in (38mm x 63mm) CLS to be a good size, but using a larger size will never hurt. Any legs must be cross-braced to prevent them from moving and opening up, which would cause serious damage to the layout and possibly the user and the room too. Trestles need to have a cord, chain or other means of securing the legs a set distance apart, or they risk doing the splits!

Where a layout is fixed around the walls, the use of a lift-up flap or a removable section should be considered to allow the operator easy access to the middle area. A lift-up flap akin to a bar counter flap should have its hinges placed on blocks that raise the hinges above rail level; then the flap will open without the rails colliding along the hinged side! The hinge packing can be a suitable timber offcut or a piece of plywood – in fact, anything that raises the hinges above rail level. Small shoot bolts hold the flap in the down position. Wiring for track feeds to the flap section should use flexible stranded wire.

Slide-out sections need to be carefully made to obtain a reasonably tight fit but still able to be slid out. Again, a small shoot bolt or two locks will fix the removable section in place. Wiring to and from the slide-out section needs to be via a multi-pin plug and socket to allow the section to be removed. Castors fitted to the bottom of the legs will allow the sliding to happen smoothly and easily.

With today's laser cutting machines, several specialist suppliers have started producing precision laser-cut baseboards. These are often supplied to the customer's own specification, both in baseboard top size and height above floor. Some kits are also supplied in 'standard' unit sizes, usually sold as 'flatpack' self-assembly units. They are very simply put together at home, much like any flatpack furniture kits. Once assembled, usually with suitable PVA glue and pins or wood screws in pre-drilled holes, the baseboard is extremely rigid and often relatively light in weight. These are ideal for modellers who do not wish to undertake the carpentry skills need to make a conventional framed baseboard or where their residence does not offer the opportunity to carry out carpentry work. These laser-cut baseboard kits are a great investment if only for the speed of assembly, let alone the simplicity of assembly.

3
Track

Our model railway will use basically three types of track: fixed sectional track pieces; flexible track lengths with matching fixed-radius points; or hand-made track and points using pieces of ready-made rail and sleepers of plastic or a copper-clad material, or even wood!

The sectional track offers immediate track usage with nothing needed other than fixing it all together and adding the power feed. It is often supplied with train sets and pieces are available as extra individual items to allow the layout to be extended. Curves are normally available in three or four pre-set and fixed radii. Normally radius 1 is the smallest or tightest curve, with radius 4 being the largest outer curved sections. Points are usually of the insulated frog (dead frog) type, offering a simple self-isolating feature towards the unset route, i.e. the unset direction is normally electrically dead and only becomes live when the point is moved over to that direction. Typical UK sectional track is produced by Hornby, by Peco in its Setrack range, and by Bachmann. Most sectional track is supplied with pre-drilled fixing holes in the sleepers. Larger-sized pins are often used and need to be either removed once ballasting is completed or their heads hidden with some suitably coloured paint to match the sleeper colouring. If removed, the holes in the sleepers can be filled with plastic moulding compound or modelling clay, or even a spot of plaster filler, then coloured with tints of paint that match the sleepers once dried. Sectional track is normally supplied with factory-fitted metal rail joiners (fishplates), two joiners per section.

Flexible track offers the advantage of forming much larger-radius curves, and normally has its parallel track centres closer together than with sectional track, e.g. in OO the sectional track centre is at 67mm, while flexible track used with the same own-brand point system provides 50mm track centres. Flexible track takes a little more skill in track-laying, as there is the need to keep the straight tracks straight and the curves to the correct chosen radius, which is often to a minimum of 24 inches, but can be tighter if wished. A steel rule placed temporarily alongside straight sections of track while pinning it in place will provide a good straight track, and the use of Tracksetta gauges can help produce an even curve. It must be noted that flexible track will require some rail cutting and probably sleeper removal and trimming off of the fixing chairs at the ends of a length where the fishplates are to be fitted. Initially, during track-laying I use very fine Peco track pins pushed into the sleepers and baseboard at intervals of 4 to 6 inches; these will aid track-laying and help keep the track in its final position until it is ballasted. I never push the fixing pins in fully, only to around half their length, then bend over their top portion onto the top of the sleeper. This makes it very easy to remove them once the track has been ballasted and all securely glued in place. I don't like seeing pin heads on my finished track!

When curving flexible track the inner rail will become longer and should be cut to match the now shorter outer rail. How you cut the rail is a personal matter, and several methods can be used: an electric mini-drill with a metal cutting disc fitted; a razor saw and a suitable block to maintain the saw upright against the block; and my personal favourite, the Xuron rail cutter, which is like a pair of wire side cutters but purely designed to cut rail cleanly on the one side. Once cut, the rails will need a light file with a flat needle file to remove any small burrs, which will aid the fitting of the rail joiner (fishplate). In addition, the rail fixing chairs on at least the first sleeper on either side of the joint will need to be removed so that the rail joiner can slide onto the rail to half its length.

Pre-curving the rails before laying can really help on curved sections of track. Slide out the rail from the chairs and carefully between thumb and first finger stroke the side of the rail, forming a gentle and even curve along the rail's length. The rail will be slightly over curved and is then carefully rethreaded back into all the sleeper chairs. Do the same with the opposite rail. By pre-curving the track it will help hold the curve. Rail joints on curves are somewhat of a pain, but by pre-curving the rails the joiner tends to maintain the curve better. If necessary, once the joiner is in place apply a slight twisting motion along its length with the aid of a pair of fine-nosed pliers. Some modellers solder their joiners to the rails on curves, but I have not found this necessary. Never solder all the rails to their joiners as some tiny movement is need inside the joiner to allow for rail expansion and contraction.

Adding ballast will enhance the layout. Ballast is available in several forms for the modeller to use; very fine real granite chippings or ground coconut shells are the main ready-made types, while home-made ballast from canary grit or aquarium gravel is just two of the alternative options. Whichever is the chosen medium, it must be sieved or produced to represent the size of typical real railway ballast stones, which are approximately 2 inches (50mm) in size. Some ballast stones are of course smaller in size and some will be a little larger, up to a maximum of around 3 inches (60mm). So, in OO scale the largest stones would be less than 1mm, and in N around 0.5mm.

Some modellers like to add a ballast shoulder, and this is often produced by laying strips of cork under the track to act as a trackbed. The thickness of the cork is dependent on the scale being worked in, but is generally between 2mm and 3mm thick. It is cut a little wider than the sleeper ends, then the edges are trimmed to a slope to represent the shoulder. Once it is bonded to the baseboard with PVA or impact adhesive, weights are applied to keep the cork flat during the glue drying period (books, paint tins or similar heavy objects can be used as weights). Once the glue has been allowed to cure, the track can be lightly pinned to the cork. The alternative (and my preferred method!) is to lay the

The three basic stages of ballasting:
1 – Track laid and tested with several locos and various items of rolling stock.
2 – Track covered with ballast of choice
3 – Track ballast teased into position with a artist-type or small paintbrush, then glued.

track directly onto the baseboard's flat surface. When using any ballast shoulder material, the modeller needs to remember that anything adjacent to the raised track needs to be raised up by the same amount, e.g. platform surfaces, goods sheds or engine sheds that locos or wagons, etc, pass through or past. All need to be raised to allow for the added rail top height caused by the cork or other material used in raising the final rail top height.

The other method of combined trackbed and ballasting is to use a proprietary foam-style trackbed, upon which the track is laid in often pre-cut sleeper indents. Most track manufactures produce a foam-type trackbed, and some are better than others. If used, the track that is laid into the foam must only be lightly pinned to stop it moving, but the pins are not inserted so hard that they press the sleepers deep into the foam and distort the track. Poor running will result if this is allowed to occur!

Once the track is laid but before ballasting, now is the time, if desired, to paint the rail sides a rusty colour. Use blended shades for rust, brown (Burnt Umber is great!) and black to vary the shading along the rails. Rusty or oily rail is not all one colour! Use a fine artist's paintbrush to apply the rusty paint colour and do not be too bothered if the paint gets onto the rail chairs as these would often be rusty too! They can always be touched in with a darker paint colour.

The actual sleepers can be painted too if wished to highlight their woodenness; on the real railway they were soaked in creosote or pitch to a dark colour before being used in the track.

If wished, apply masking tape along the outer edges of the trackbed – the cess area – to prevent overspray if painting sleepers or rails and; it can be used for the ballasting to give a neat edge to the ballast.

Having made the choice of ballast material, the modeller needs to ensure that it cannot be sucked up into any passing locomotive's gearing, which if allowed would cause serious mechanical failure. The ballast therefore must be glued in position. There are two methods of doing this. The first and possibly the most

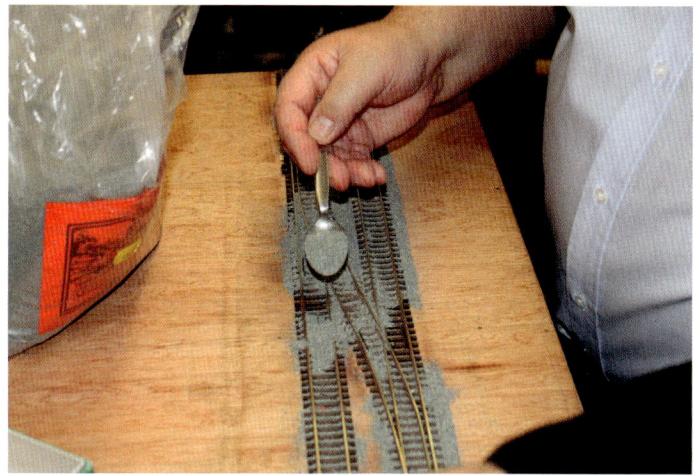

A teaspoon is used as a 'ballast shovel', then the ballast is moved into its final position with the aid of a soft-bristle brush. Here a paintbrush is being used for the initial ballast placement, then a smaller artist's brush to get the final correct finish.

basic is to apply a band of neat PVA glue to the trackbed or baseboard before laying the track, then, as soon as the track is lightly pinned down, sprinkle the ballast between the sleepers and along the two outside shoulders, brushing away surplus ballast as you work along the pre-glued area. The second method, and favoured by myself, as I feel it gives a far better result, is to lay the track, wire it, test-run several locos and trains, then make good any problems noted by using pieces of thin card shims placed under the track to lift up any low areas. Once all is proved to be satisfactory, sprinkle the dry ballast along the track centre and outside edges – use a teaspoon as a mini 'shovel' to place the ballast if wished. Then, with the aid of a 1-inch (20-25mm) paintbrush and a smaller artist's brush, move the dry ballast around until the correct profile is obtained on the outer edges and the middle of the track is correctly ballasted.

Once you are happy with the look of the ballast, take a plant mister bottle or other suitable clean mister-style bottle – a well-washed-out former kitchen surface spray bottle is ideal – fill with tap water and add some Isopropanol (Isopropyl) Alcohol – known as IPA – at a strength of 99.9%, or use methylated spirit (meths) if IPA isn't readily available, mixing it to about 90% water/10% IPA or meths. Gently spray all the dry ballast to make it wet; the IPA or meths will act as a wetting agent, reducing the surface tension and causing the water to seep into the ballast better. Now mix PVA glue with tap water and a few drops of the IPA or meths in a container. The strongest mix is 50/50 glue to water, but the glue can be diluted much more with water if desired, to around 75/25 water to glue, then add the IPA or meths to the mix – you only need to add a little. With the aid of an eye-dropper or pipette, apply the glue mix to the ballast, allowing it to soak into every part. Ensure that no glue is allowed into the tie bar or any other moving part of a set of points. Also watch out for the thinned glue mix running out through baseboard wiring holes and joints and dropping onto the best Axminster carpet! Best practice prior to starting is to lay down some temporary sheets of plastic under the layout where there is a risk of a carpet or flooring being damaged!

Once the glue mix has been applied, leave the baseboard and glued ballast alone. Don't poke at it or try to move anything once it has been glued. With a clean lint-free cloth dampened with a little of the IPA or meths, gently wipe over the rail tops to remove any glue deposits. Allow at least a full 24 hours, then carefully vacuum off any unstuck ballast – there will always be a few little spots that didn't fully glue and will come up under the vacuum's suction! Once vacuumed, go back over the area and touch in any bald areas with more ballast, then apply a few drops of the PVA/glue/IPA mix to bond these areas in place. Again leave for a full 24 hours and vacuum again to remove any remaining loose particles.

Once the ballast is correct, gently overspray it with a water and IPA or meths mix, then diluted PVA is added from an eye-dropper or pipette, or a small bottle with a fine applicator nozzle.

Safety: When using IPA or methylated spirit, always ensure that you have adequate ventilation in the room and observe all safety issues – no naked flame or smoking, etc!

Some modellers prefer to use a latex adhesive, as used in the fitting of carpets and vinyl flooring. This is diluted with water as per the PVA glue to the required consistency, and a few drops of IPA or meths can be added. Latex allows easier removal of the glued ballast and track should the track plan be changed later on.

After 24 hours or more your track should be bonded securely in place. The extra-fine track pins previously inserted through the sleepers can now be carefully pulled out and discarded. Clean the rail tops to remove all traces of the glue mix. Use a track rubber, an ultra-fine-grit emery cloth or a fibre pencil if you have one of sufficient width to clean the rail tops. Follow up with a final clean using a lint-free cloth dampened with a little neat 99.9% IPA or meths to remove any final residue and ensure the rails are spotlessly clean.

An example of finished ballasting, where additional scenic scatters have been added to enhance the overall scene.

4
Wiring

Wiring is perhaps most disliked by many modellers for fear of the unknown! However, when taken piece by piece, wire by wire, it can become much easier to understand and work with.

Firstly, let's look at the type of wire used. Conventionally it is made from a copper conductor, as copper is an excellent conductor of electricity. The copper wire needs to be isolated from coming into contact with other copper wires, so today most wire is wrapped in a PVC jacket or sleeve, as PVC is a great insulator. Other insulating mediums are used, but PVC is one of the most commonly found types.

Our wire comes in two types: solid conductor, or flexible strands making up the overall conductor. Which is best? Answer – both! It really depends on what the wire is being used for. For example, if the model railway is a portable layout that is moved from room to room or even taken to exhibitions, etc, then using solid wires may well lead to the wires eventually fracturing due to continual movement; flexible wires should be able to cope far better in this situation. Layouts may use a mix of both solid and flexible wires. An example is a fixed home layout that is using Digital Command Control (DCC); ideally a DCC track feed bus pair of wires is installed and smaller dropper wires connect the bus wire to the rail above. The bus pair can be of solid wire while the droppers can be flexible wire. There are no hard and fast rules, and the bus may just as easily be made from flexible wire! Just use the wire that is most suitable for the job for which it is needed. If the wire is going to move and flex frequently or needs to bend sharply around an obstacle, consider a flexible wire as the most suitable.

By now I can already hear the groans about 'bus' and 'dropper' wires being mentioned! Well, let us talk briefly about them to ease the mind! A 'bus' is nothing more than a means of connecting power to a main feed wire – the bus wire. Generally two separate wires make up a bus pair, and these are often referred to simply as the bus. The main feed distribution device is the bus wire, which runs around the layout or wherever it is needed, providing a good low-resistance path for power to where it is required. A simple bus can be nothing more than a pair of wires used to provide layout lighting, and all road, building and platform lights are connected to this bus pair of wires. The bus is fed at one end by a suitable power source and at the far end it is terminated somehow to stop the two wire ends touching each other. Along the length of the bus wire smaller 'dropper' wires drop down from all the lights, etc, that need to be connected to the bus pair.

'Droppers' are normally of a smaller wire size than the bus wires. This is because each dropper wire only carries a small amount of power in amperes to whatever it feeds – e.g. a street light. Each street light is rated at, say, 70 milliamps (0.07A) for a filament lit lamp. Several lights may be connected to the lighting bus pair and when power is applied the total consumption of this power in amperes is what is flowing in the bus pair. Assume there are 20 lights, so 20 times 0.07 is 1.4 amps. This power is all carried in the bus pair of wires, hence the need for them to be larger in size than the fine dropper wires leading to each of the lights – we don't want the bus glowing in the darkness under the baseboard due to it being too small a wire size! A very serious enemy of the bus pair is a voltage drop; this occurs due to the resistance of the wire used. The larger the wire size, the lower its resistance and the less the voltage drop will be for a set distance. After all, we don't want to feed 12 volts in at the source only to have 9 or fewer volts under load at the far end! However, volt drop really only becomes a serious problem on longer wire runs.

What type of wire for what circuit? This question is asked many times and the answer is – use what is suitable! Modellers are often very good at saving the pennies! But at times scrimping at the wiring installation stage doesn't result in a saving later on when problems start to occur and the wiring has to be replaced! Telephone wire, bell wire and small fine speaker wire are often used. However, in the main these really are not that suitable for use over any reasonable distance due to our old enemy volt drop! They all have very fine wires designed for low current applications.

Below are some tried and tested examples of minimum wire sizing and their use in model railways. My apologies to those not UK-based who may not understand fully the metric wire sizing, but I have attempted to give the approximate AWG (American Wire Gauge) sizes as well, although direct conversion isn't always that accurate.

Bus wires for DCC layouts: minimum 32/0.2mm or 1.0mm^2 (17AWG)
Bus wires for layout lighting up to 3.0A: 16/0.2mm or 0.5mm^2 (20AWG)
Droppers for rail feeding DCC over 400mm in total length rail to bus: 16/0.2mm, 0.5mm^2 (20AWG)
Droppers for rail feeding DCC not exceeding 300mm in total length rail to bus: 7/0.2mm, 0.2mm^2 (24AWG)
DC rail feeding not exceeding 4 metres: 7/0.2mm, 0.20mm^2 (24AWG)
DC rail feeding exceeding 4 metres: 16/0.2mm, 0.5mm^2 (20AWG)
Solenoid point motor wiring not exceeding 4 metres: 16/0.2mm, 0.5mm^2 (20AWG)
Common return wiring: 32/0.2mm, 1.0mm^2 (17AWG)
Stall-style point motor wiring: 7/0.2mm, 0.20mm^2 (24AWG)
Colour light signal wiring using LEDs: 7/0.2mm, 0.20mm^2 (24AWG)
Layout building and street lighting, etc: 16/0.2mm, 0.5mm^2 (20AWG) for the main feeds, and finer wires to the lights

These examples are the minimum I recommend for each application to give trouble-free results. You can always install larger-sized wire without ever causing issues.

What is meant by '32/0.2mm'? This is the number of individual wires that make up the conductor and their actual wire size. Thus 32/0.2 has 32 individual wires each of 0.2mm in size, while 7/0.2 has just seven wires each of 0.2mm. These types of wire are normally referred to as their size (7/0.2, etc), and often the words 'Equipment' or 'Hook-up' wire are used.

Be a little cautious of some hobby/model shops or retailers selling so-called 'Layout wire'; this is quite often the smaller 7/0.2mm equipment wire and may not be suitable for some wiring jobs! So always ask what the actual wire size is.

A question often asked is – are there any fixed rules for wiring insulation colour? The answer is that there is no fixed colour code – modellers can choose the colours they find adequate for the job. Red and black are popular for denoting a DC feed and return, and any colours can be used for point control. (Frequently on pre-wired solenoid motors red, green and black are used, but their colour coded function differs between manufacturers.) DCC bus feeds and droppers to the rails can be in any two colours of your choice, e.g. brown and blue. The most important thing to do is to try and keep the same wiring colour code throughout the layout or confusion may well occur at a later date if and when a problem arises.

What is the best way to make wire connections? Without doubt the very best connection is one that has been correctly soldered. A soldered joint that has been correctly made will virtually never fail, although the emphasis has to be on 'correctly made' – see the paragraphs further on regarding soldering. Another type of connection is one that is twisted and insulated, and while this works it is not the best option as eventually the joint can become loose and a high-resistance joint then occurs, resulting in much head-scratching trying to find the problem. My advice therefore is not to use this method. Screw-down terminal blocks, sometimes called 'choc blocks', make secure and quick connections and allow differing sizes of wires to be joined together. Make sure the terminal connector used is not too large for the wires being connected into it. If at all possible choose terminal block connectors that use a small thin metal finger inside the connector and the grub screw pushes the finger down onto the wire, rather than the more conventional type where the grub screw itself tightens and twists down onto the wire, which can lead to wire distortion and even wire fracture!

Another method is to use 'suitcase' connectors sometimes called Scotchlok (the maker's name). These work by displacing and severing the wire insulation as an internal notched V blade is pushed down, making contact onto the copper wire. The down side is that most need the two wires being joined to be roughly of the same size, though there are connectors that do allow for differing wire sizes to be joined. Some of these connectors have a tap-off connection onto which a 'push-on' spade-style connector fits, thereby allowing differing wire sizes to be connected together. Suitcase connectors tend to come in three main sizes, denoted by their body colour: yellow (the largest connector) has wire size connections of around 2.5mm^2 to 6.0mm^2; blue has 1.0mm^2 to 2.5mm^2; and red is 0.4mm^2 to 1.0mm^2. Note that the wire sizes stated may differ between manufacturers. It is important to obtain the correct colour-coded suitcase connector to fit the wires that need to be joined. Using the wrong size can lead to the wires being cut through or the connector being too loose.

Recently, sprung-grip push-in-style terminal blocks are gaining popularity and these often come in two-, three- and five-way groups, with all terminals in that group interconnected. One such make is Wago, but there are others.

To make a soldered joint in wiring I recommend the use of 60/40 Rosen cored solder, which has a special flux suitable for electrical connection built in. Lead-free solder is now taking over from lead content 60/40 solder, but this does need a higher temperature at which to solder, and some older soldering irons are not quite able to fully reach the necessary temperature. I do not recommend adding any additional flux to electrical joints – it is not really necessary. Whatever you do, avoid fluxes sold for general-purpose soldering work, as these will contain acid and they need to be washed off after the soldering is completed. This of course is not possible with an electrical joint. There are some fluxes sold specifically for electrical work and these can be used if wished.

The choice of soldering iron is fairly important. If you have an old iron with a battered bit, it is probably time to replace it with a modern iron! Modern soldering iron tips are coated with a special metal surface to prolong bit life and should never be filed. Only use a damp sponge to wipe the iron's tip. If the tip is seen to become coated in what can only be called 'surface crud', then consider using a special soldering iron tip reviver/cleaner, often made with brass particles or a paste to clean the tip. Never file it! The choice of iron will depend on what you are going to solder. For most general electrical soldering work on a model railway a 25 watt iron will suffice. However, a higher-wattage iron will never hurt – in fact, it can be an advantage at times as the tip's temperature will be maintained or replaced faster as the heat is sucked out by whatever the iron is in direct contact with.

Tip shape is a personal choice, but I like a single-angled chisel tip, with a tapered pointed tip coming a close second. Tip size is also a fairly important factor – too large and you will not be able to use it easily in small confined places, while too small and you do not get the transfer of heat rapidly, making soldering virtually impossible. Some irons allow their tips to be interchanged; Antex is one such manufacturer, but there are others. A soldering iron safety stand is really an essential item, as it keeps the hot iron's tip secure and normally comes with a built-in sponge tip-cleaning pad.

To make the joint you need to ensure that the two items to be soldered are spotlessly clean. Freshly stripped wire will be clean, but if left exposed to the air for several hours or longer it will start to tarnish and will benefit from cleaning. Rail to be soldered or to have wires attached to it should always be cleaned in the area of soldering, even if it is new track from the box. I like to use a fibre pencil for this cleaning process, but a piece of emery cloth or a craft knife blade could also be used, but do be careful if using a knife blade as a scraper as it is all too easy to damage the wire!

To join two wires together after they have been cleaned or are freshly stripped, twist them together to form a tight but dry joint. Let the soldering iron reach full temperature – allow 5 minutes from switching it on. Wipe the tip on the damp sponge, then apply the Rosen corded solder to the tip, coating the tip in molten solder. Place the coated iron's tip onto the joint and allow a few seconds for the heat to transfer into the wires. Then feed the end of the cored solder onto the heated wire joint and allow the solder to melt and flow into and around the joint. Remove the iron and don't move the joint for at least 5 to 7 seconds, or until the solder is seen to take on a dull sheen as it sets. Wipe the soldering iron tip on the damp sponge and place the iron back in the safety stand.

To solder a dropper wire to a rail I recommend pre-coating the wire with solder – called 'tinning'. As before, heat the iron and once it is at full temperature and the wire has been freshly stripped to remove approximately 4mm to 5mm of insulation and, if required, bent into an 'L' shape, wipe the iron's tip on the damp sponge and apply a coating of solder to the tip. Hold the tip onto the bare wire and feed the end of the solder onto the heated wire, coating the whole bare wire in solder. Wipe the tip on the sponge and place the iron in its holder. Clean the rail surface where the soldering is to occur, then place the iron with a fresh coating of solder on its tip onto the rail. Once the hot tip has heated the rail (a couple of seconds usually) feed the cored solder onto the rail and the iron's tip where it is held against the rail; when the solder is seen to flow onto the rail, remove the iron. Now place the tinned wire into its final position against the tinned rail. Apply a fresh coating of solder to the iron's tip and hold the iron against the wire, pressing it against the rail. Allow a couple of seconds for the heat to transfer from the iron into the wire, then into the rail. If necessary, angle the iron's tip so that it is touching both the rail and the wire. Also if necessary, feed the end of the cored solder onto the wire and allow it to flow onto the rail. Once the rail and wire solders are seen to melt into one, remove the iron and maintain the joint in place. Wipe the tip on the sponge and place it in the safety stand. Note that as soon as the iron's tip is removed the wire can be held in place by a flat-bladed screwdriver or tweezers, etc, to avoid movement of the joint. Allow the joint to cool before attempting to move the wire if it has to be moved.

These two rail feed dropper wires have been soldered to the underside of the rails prior to track-laying. The two wires pass down through the baseboard surface via a single hole drilled roughly in the middle of the track – this allows final side-to-side adjustment of the track. The two triangle marks denote the rail feed and return (the open triangle for a feed and the solid triangle for the return), so that the track polarity is maintained correctly. Once test trains are run to prove all is correct, the track can be ballasted and the ballast will hide the dropper wires, making the connections invisible.

5
Train control

The two main methods used currently are DC (analogue) and DCC (digital). AC control also exists, but is now very much being replaced by these two methods.

For many years our model railways were operated by analogue control – DC (Direct Current). This works by applying a variable DC voltage to the rails; typically the voltage varies between 0 (zero) volts and the maximum, which is a nominal 12 volts. The more volts applied to the rails the faster the locomotive moves, as the electric motor inside the loco increases its revolutions in line with the volts being fed to it.

In the early days of ready-made off-the-shelf train sets, the speed control was from dry cells – batteries – with a simple set of resistances connected in series with the output to provide slow and medium speed settings and the full battery volts fed to the rails when the controller was in the third maximum speed setting. To reverse the direction of travel the output polarity was swapped around, that is positive on one rail being replaced by negative and the opposite on the other rail, causing the electric motor to turn the other way.

In the 1930s to 1950s more UK homes changed their mains power from DC to AC (Alternating Current) and mains-powered controllers became more common. Inside their casing is an isolating transformer that reduces the mains 240 volts to around 16 volts AC, and electrically isolates the lethal 240-volt mains power from the low-voltage outputs. For train control the 16-volt AC is fed into a device called a bridge rectifier, and this converts the AC into DC, a small amount of voltage being lost in the process. The DC is then fed onto one end of a large resistance mat, and a wiper arm moves in an arc or up and down over the mat. The arm's movement is controlled by turning the speed control knob on the front or top of the controller. As the speed knob is moved from the off position towards the full-speed position, less and less resistance is inserted into the output by the wiper arm moving over the resistance mat, until eventually at full speed no resistance is left in circuit and the full 12 volts flow out to the rails and the loco's motor. Note that 12 volts is nominal and may be higher if read on a multimeter. Being a variable resistance, much finer speed control can be obtained compared with the earlier three-speed step controller. It should be noted that the three-step controller continued in production alongside the variable controller, and three-step mains-powered controllers were supplied in train sets for many years.

With the advent of the transistor the variable resistance mat controller became virtually redundant, as now there was no need for it or the wiper arm. Speed control is now arranged from a small low-power 'volume'-type potentiometer, which allows the transistors to be turned on by varying their control volts, which in turn allows larger voltages and current to be passed by the output transistors. Controllers of this style will use a power transistor in the main output, while smaller lower-powered transistors feed the larger power transistor, varying the output set by the position of the speed knob. Today many DC controllers have moved away from direct power feeding to what is called Pulse Width Modulation (PWM) control. Here full voltage is available all the time that the speed setting is on, but it is only fed to the output and rails in microsecond bursts, with 'off' gaps in between the 'on' periods. The time length of the 'on' to 'off' gaps. or spaces in the output. determines how fast the motor will turn for a given pulse/space ratio. For example, for full power the full 12 volts is allowed to pass out to the rails, even though in reality there are likely to be some very small 'off' periods in the output, but they are so small that they can be discounted. To allow our loco to move at half speed, the full power to the rails is turned 'on' and 'off' in equal spacings. For quarter-speed running the power is turned 'off' for longer than the 'on' period. All this is occurring at a very high speed or frequency, so the motor, while receiving full voltage with every 'on' pulse, only ever rotates at the setting provided, due to the 'off' periods interrupting the supply. This works very well with most locomotive motors, but some do not like PWM and can overheat; this particularly applies to coreless motors. Therefore the modeller will have to revert to the transistor-controlled type of train speed controller. But in the main most locomotive motors produced today are happy to work with PWM, as this is how DCC loco decoders feed their motors!

Cab control

With cab control wiring, a DC layout using two (or more) separate DC controllers is divided into several electrically isolated sections called 'blocks', or sometimes 'cab sections'. Each block is independent of all the others, so a train in Block A can be operated by Controller 1, and a train in Block B can be operated by Controller 2. Equally, each block can be fed from Controller 1 or Controller 2 depending on the position of the cab switch for that block.

Each block starts and ends with an IRJ (Insulated Rail Joiner), or a narrow slit cut through the same-handed rail. While a cab-controlled layout looks like a continuous track, electrically it is composed of several separate track sections.

An operator using Controller 1 sets the block switch to his or her controller – Cab A – and moves the locomotive through that one block. Approaching the next block, he uses another switch to connect the second block to Controller 1. Now the two blocks are electrically connected to Cab A and the locomotive moves from the first block into the second. Just before the loco enters a third block, the operator connects the new block to Cab A. Following this pattern, the operator can move the loco from one end of a layout to the other.

While this is happening, a second operator using Cab B can drive his or her locomotive elsewhere on the layout simply by connecting the blocks being used to Cab B. In this manner, the two operators can follow each other around a layout, turning the cab switches to align the blocks to the control cabs A or B as needed.

The only downside to cab control is that two locomotives cannot share the same block at the same time. Operator B must wait until operator A has cleared a block in order to switch the track power in that block from Cab A to Cab B.

Single Pole Double Throw (SPDT) and, ideally, centre-off-type switches connect one cab to a specific block at a time, but there's no option available for both operators to connect their individual controllers to the same block at the same time. The only time when problems can occur is if operator A allows their train to pass over the IRJs into the section that's being controlled by operator B.

A very simplistic section of track is shown later, which has been divided up into several sections or blocks by the IRJs (Insulated Rail Joiners) or gaps cut through the rail, and the two cabs (controllers) are only permitted to feed the section of track depending on the position of that section's cab switch. Either A or B adding a central-off switch position allows isolation of that section.

Note that if DC controllers use a common return wiring method then these controllers *must* be fed from totally separate power supplies or via separate windings on a dual-wound transformer – see the drawing overleaf. You cannot use one power source to feed more than one controller. If you do not wish to use DC common return wiring, replace the SPDT switches with DPDT switches and feed both track feeds from each controller to each side of each switch. The positive would be the same as for common return – just add the returns

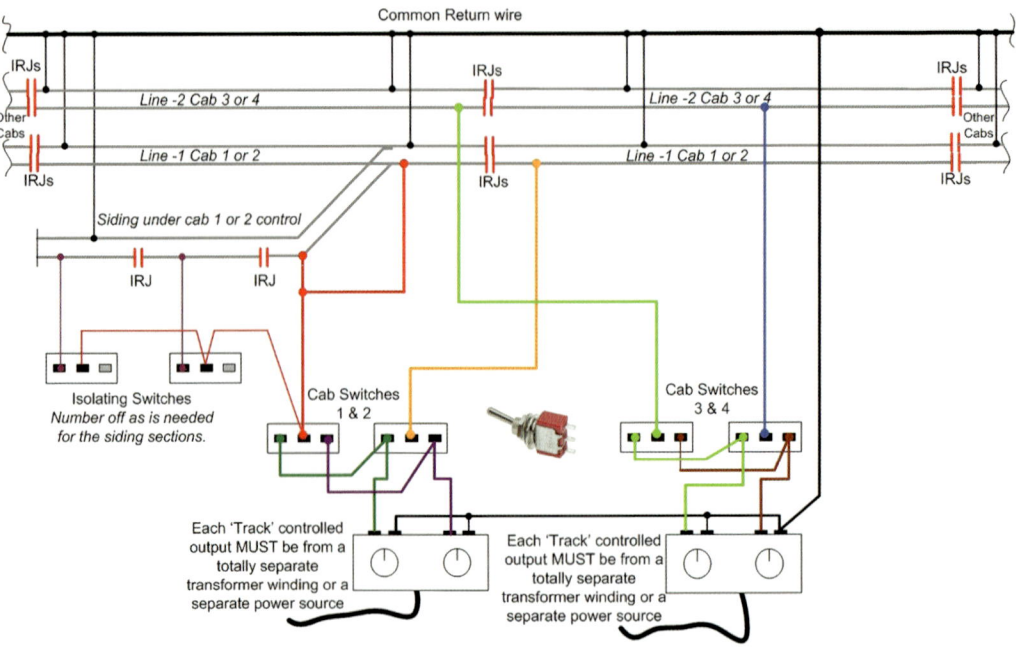

to the switches rather than commoning them together.

DCC (Digital Command Control)

This is the second most commonly used system. Still reasonably new to many in the UK, this method of control has been around for a couple of decades at the time of writing! As the name suggests, digital information is sent to the locomotives and lineside accessories – but nothing will work if it is directly connected to the DCC rails! 'Decoders' are needed to interface between the DCC supply and the device to be operated, be it a locomotive's motor or an accessory such as a point motor or signal. There are two basic types of decoder: mobile, as used in locomotives and carriages, etc, and static. Static decoders, usually called 'Accessory Decoders', are normally fitted to the layout's baseboard and operate accessories such as point motors. The decoder is basically an interface device that receives digital commands sent from the DCC base unit and converts the commands into analogue outputs to power electric motors or light lamps, etc. DCC layouts usually have all rails fully powered all the time.

Isolating sections or points that self-isolate are not required to allow DCC to work to its full potential. With all tracks live, loco lights or sounds can be left on even with the points controlling that track set for a different route. Thus shunting can be undertaken in a group of sidings with the points still set for the main line.

An example of how DCC works is that each item connected to the DCC system is given a unique 'address number', set by the user, between 1 and 9999. Only when that unique number is sent as part of a coded sequence or broadcast from the DCC base or command unit will that decoder act upon the next stream of information to be sent in that broadcast. All other decoders, while connected and 'listening' to what is being sent, will ignore it, as their unique address number hasn't been sent in the broadcast – so they remain doing whatever they were told to do last time their broadcast was sent; for example, it might be stopped, running or powering some other device. It should be noted that some basic or budget ranges of DCC systems only allow a small amount of address numbers to be used. Please also note

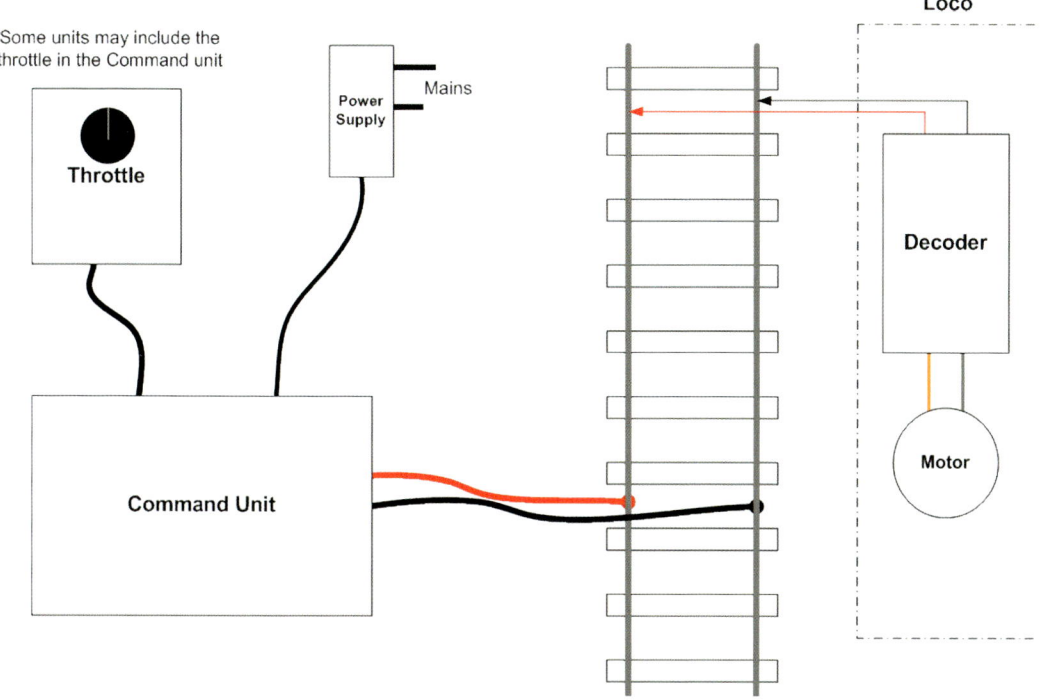

DCC control

that new loco decoders are all pre-set to address number 03, and the user should change this to something else as soon as possible – if two new decoder-fitted locos are placed on the rails with the same address number both will move together under that one address number.

Put very simply, think of DCC addressing as like a postman on his round delivering a letter with instructions in it. There are up to 9999 houses in the street. The postman only puts the letter through No 38's letterbox (the unique address in this case) and the occupant of No 38 reads the instruction and acts upon it. All the other house numbers, 1 to 37 and 39 to 9999, have seen the postman on his rounds but haven't got the letter, so they carry on doing what they were last doing! But No 38 now does something different.

The introduction of wi-fi train and accessory control via a smart phone or tablet is becoming increasingly popular with some DCC users and free-to-use downloaded applications for most mobile phones or tablets are available. Wi-fi connections to the DCC command system are either via the home internet router, or a dedicated router that connects directly to the DCC system are now available. The MRC/Gaugemaster Prodigy wi-fi system is one such system.

The MRC/Gaugemaster Prodigy wi-fi system.

A third system and relatively new to the model railway scene is full Bluetooth control. Each locomotive has an onboard Bluetooth decoder fitted, much like DCC. An 'app' (application) is downloaded from the internet to a smartphone, tablet or other smart device with Bluetooth capability. The smart device communicates directly with the loco's decoder via Bluetooth radio signals and control of the loco is via a throttle control on the smart device. There is virtually no limit to the number of Bluetooth locos or other devices that can be controlled, so long as each has a unique address number or other reference detail. Bluetooth control is still very much in its infancy at the time of writing, but it is looking to become a serious contender in model railway train control by wi-fi. Bluetooth uses a continuous voltage applied to the rails, and the Bluetooth decoder uses this voltage to control whatever it is connected to, as it receives commands that are sent wirelessly by the controlling device. There is no need for a router, computer or any other peripheral items to allow the Bluetooth device to connect to the Bluetooth decoder fitted in the loco or somewhere on the baseboard.

As previously mentioned, the DC or analogue controller varies the volts on the rails (between nominally 0 and 12 volts) while DCC has full voltage on the rails continually (nominally 12 to 16 volts AC). With DCC you drive all the individual locos on the same track, while with DC you normally only drive one loco per controller per track.

Which is best – DC or DCC? Well, neither system is better than the other! DC has a well-established following and has a proven record. DCC is making serious inroads into the hobby and now has a good following with currently a significant percentage of all new train set sales being DCC capable.

Basically a DC system needs one controller per loop or running line. This gives better control of each line and allows two or more locos to run, each under the control of their own dedicated DC controller. To hold locos in platforms or sidings, isolating sections of track are installed and their rails connected to on/off switches.

Many consider changing from DC to DCC but are put off by the high cost of having to install DCC decoders in all of their DC locos. It isn't always necessary to convert all of them all at once – convert three or four at a time or as your budget allows, keeping the non-converted locos in isolated sidings or completely off the DCC-powered rails until they are converted. Only convert those that run faultlessly on DC power, as converting a poor DC running loco will result in it becoming far worse on DCC! Either service a poor running DC loco and retry it on DC to see if it is now a faultless runner, or sell it and put the money gained towards the cost of a new DCC-ready or DCC-fitted loco. If you can't part with it, put it in a display case!

DC control

How does DC work? A variable speed and direction of travel controller is used to vary the voltage supplied to the rails. These controllers come in ready-made units with one, two, three or four controllers fitted into the one case, or they can be of the hand-held type, where just one controller is used. Many controllers will offer auxiliary power outlets to feed lighting, point motors, etc. These auxiliary outputs are normally 12 volts DC and 16 volts AC. Most N, OO and HO controllers will provide around a 1.0-ampere output to the track terminals, while larger-gauge controllers will provide substantially more current (ampere) output. Each controller will have its own pair of 'Track' terminals or pre-fitted track feed wires, and these allow the power to be connected to the rails from the controller's terminals or direct from the controller. By varying the speed control knob or switch, the track output voltage is varied. Direction of travel is altered by a switch or a centre-off speed knob, where turning the knob one way produces forward travel and, after passing through the centre off position to the other direction, varies the speed in the opposite direction of travel. But many controllers today will use a single-speed knob and a separate direction-of-travel switch.

Forward direction on DC is gained by applying a positive voltage to the right-hand rail – that is the rail beneath the right-hand side of the locomotive when looking along the loco towards the chimney. To reverse a DC locomotive the power to the rails is swapped around, resulting in the electric motor turning in the opposite direction.

The locomotive's wheels collect the power in the rails and transfer it to the electric motor inside the model. The motor will turn faster the more voltage is applied to the rails from the controller. The motor then turns a gear train, which ultimately turns the driving wheels, thereby producing the movement forward or backwards.

Connections to the rail are made in several ways, perhaps by plug-in power clips to power track sections. Probably the very best way is by soldering the feed wire directly to the rail. Ideally, solder the wire to the underside of the rail before laying the track; however, if the track is already laid, soldering the feed wire to the rail's outer web area will be the second-best option. Take the feed wires below the baseboard via small drilled holes.

From DC to DCC

With DCC, full rail volts are applied to the rails all the time and are transferred to the locomotive's decoder. A digital signal is also carried in the rail power. The decoder acts upon the digital commands issued to it and uses the full rail power to drive the motor by using the Pulse Width Modulation method of motor control, as discussed earlier. Lighting and other separately controllable features are also provided by the decoder, again using the full rail voltage, but converted to DC. To reverse a DCC locomotive the decoder swaps around the feed to the motor, while the rail power remains always the same. Also, it is AC.

A question often asked is, 'My layout is DC – how do I convert it to DCC?' In the simplest form, take all the controller wires off the DC controller's 'Track' terminals and connect them together into two bunches, ensuring that all wires going to the left-hand rails are together and all the wires going to the right-hand rails are together. Connect the now pairs of wires to the 'Track' output of a DCC control system. If you have isolating sections, turn on all the isolating switches. Your layout, if wired correctly, should now work on DCC. Ensure that all your locos have decoders fitted.

If your DC layout uses analogue point operation for the solenoid motors, can they still be used? Yes of course. There is no reason why analogue point motor operation cannot be used with the DCC just operating the locos. You will need a suitable power supply to feed the motors and the passing contact levers or switches, but that is all. However, do keep analogue wires, controls and operations totally separate from all DCC wiring.

Will points need to be modifying for DCC operation? No. There is really no such thing as a DCC point. If the point works on DC rail power, it will do the same on DCC. There are things that can be done to improve the point for both DCC and DC! Adding rail feeds to the points' two outside stock rails will ensure that power and data for DCC are directly fed to the point. Installing additional rail feeds after the point will ensure that the self-isolating feature of points will be overcome. Or if your points are Hornby examples, fitting two Hornby Electro point clips (R8232) per point will overcome the points' self-isolating feature for the DCC user.

6
Construction kits

Kits have for many years been the backbone of model railway rolling stock and buildings. Traditionally made from card, plastic or wood, today laser-cut wooden and card kits are rapidly expanding. Kits are generally fairly simple to put together and provide a great range of buildings, locos, wagons and carriages, and virtually all types of model railway scales are catered for.

Today there is also a vast range of cast resin ready-built and painted buildings available. But why leave your buildings to look like hundreds of other similar examples?

Enhancing a kit or a ready-made resin building beyond its basic form is a really good way of improving and individualising it. Adding additional small detailing parts to the structure, either purchased or hand-made, will really improve the building. There are many suppliers of additional detailing components, or you could even use parts left over from other kits or parts recovered from older dismantled buildings. Many ready-made detailing parts are made from plastic, white metal and brass; perhaps the white metal and brass examples are the better choice for providing fine detail. But modern plastic detailing parts now hold their own too.

The simplest forms of added detailing are

- new and various-sized chimney pots
- lead flashing around the chimney stack or roof joints
- guttering and down pipes together with the down pipe wall fixings
- waste water pipes for WCs, sinks or baths in the building
- 'S'- or 'X'-shaped wall tie bracing plates often found on older buildings
- street name plates on the corners of buildings, etc.

On steam locos, tools such as fire irons and shovels, and oil lamps to show the designation of the train or loco – e.g. Fast Passenger, Stopping Passenger, Goods, etc – all add to the realism, not forgetting the crew in the cab who drive the train!

Weathering a building or rolling stock item will enhance it more. Weathering is adding those streaks of dirty colour that are seen on real buildings and items of rolling stock, such as staining running down the wall from an overflow pipe or leaking down pipe. General road dirt splashes onto the lower levels of a building where heavy traffic passes by, and railway brake dust film collects on locos, etc.

Domestic buildings can benefit from garden detail. Boundary fencing and gates together with garden details, such as a lawn, borders with flowers, and paths with drain and manhole inspection pit covers, all add that little extra detail.

Some card kits can have their windows replaced by etched brass frets, which provide a greater level of detail than the 'as supplied' transparent plastic printed window frames. Even if etched parts are not readily available, by using fine plastic microstrip frames and other window detail can be constructed.

Adding internal detail to rooms will make a building look lived-in or, where a commercial property is represented, at least look used and inviting. Adding people to carriage interiors will improve their look – far better than running empty trains!

Domestic rooms can be easily constructed from painted card, or use some of the readily available pre-printed sheets or downloadable sheets of interior detail. Scalescene.com is one such supplier, which produces sheets for those who wish to print them off themselves.

Commercial properties can be made to look more realistic by adding extra detail. Shop windows can be enhanced by using printed items from real commercial adverts. For example, visiting an electrical retailer's website might produce many pictures of washing machines, TVs, fridges, etc, which can be copied and reduced in size to suit the scale, then carefully cut out and arranged to look as though the window is actually containing these items. Periodical magazines offer another good selection, but getting the correct scale size may prove a little difficult unless a photocopier or scanner is used to reduce them. Try to aim for a semi-3D effect, by not only copying the flat front view but adding side and top detail to make the appliance or item stand out. Offices could contain filling cabinets, desks and even computer monitors, especially where a modern office is being depicted. Again much of this detail can be taken or copied from magazines or downloaded from web pages, etc.

A quick note on using and copying items – as long as your model is not going to be displaying a particular real-life manufacturer, retailer's name or other trade mark that can be clearly distinguished, there should not be any problems in copying or using the items. If you believe there could be a copyright issue, contact the original owner of the picture and ask permission to use it, explaining that you wish to use the picture in a model building and not for trade or any other use; 99 times out of 100 they will be more than happy for you to use their pictures. But please don't just copy a product picture then openly use it to show brand names, especially where a model may be on the exhibition circuit or used in photographic settings for any commercial or other financial gain.

By adding some lighting to the interiors of buildings you can then see the interior detail through the windows. However, do be cautious of using filament lamps inside buildings as these get very hot in use and can easily melt or soften plastic! LEDs (Light Emitting Diodes) offer a good level of illumination, but do ensure that those used are either warm or sunny white types. Many so-called 'white' LEDs are in fact tinged with blue and can give a very strange-looking level of illumination. In fact, all white LEDs are basically blue and they have phosphors added to give the white light. The use of LED strips is also a boon to illuminate the insides of buildings. These often come in strips of three or multiples of three with very small surface-mounted LEDs together with a series resistor all on the one strip. Applying 12 volts DC to the strip's connection pads the correct way round immediately provides great internal lighting.

However, do not illuminate every room. Ensure that there are some rooms unlit, achieving this by fitting internal walls, floors and ceilings to act as separators to prevent light spreading from area to area. Paint the inside faces of any external walls black or a suitable dark colour to prevent any light bleeding through the walls.

Before starting to construct a kit or your own building from scratch, you will need some basic tools. I recommend the following be obtained as a minimum:

- self-healing cutting mat
- scalpel or craft knife with spare blades – you'll use plenty of blades
- 12-inch (300mm) steel rule or safety rule
- engineer's square, 120mm or 150mm type
- small scissors – I find nail scissors ideal
- suitable adhesive for the medium being used, e.g. PVA glue or specialist glue for gluing cardboard
- needle files or a fine grade of glass paper
- solvent weld for plastics
- superglue (cyanoacrylate, also known as cyano) for bonding etched parts if they are not soldered together, and the cyano for bonding etched parts to the building structure
- small artist's paint brush for applying the solvent weld adhesive
- suitable coffee mug

No, it is not time for a cup of tea! The mug is used for the solvent weld bottle. It keeps it more stable and helps prevent it being accidentally knocked over, which will almost certainly happen if the bottle is left free standing and opened!

Some other 'nice to have' tools are:

- small sheet (approximately 300mm x 300mm) of 6mm or thicker float glass or a similar-sized mirror to be used as a level surface to build on. **Important:** get your local glass merchant to bevel all the edges
- razor saw with suitable handle
- pin vice drill and selection of small drill bits
- wooden cocktail sticks
- heavy-duty utility knife with spare blades and masking tape

Making a start with kit construction

Always read the instruction leaflet, then read it again! Carefully check all the parts of the kit against the list of parts or any other detailed item listing. Once you have ascertained that all the component parts are present, ensure that all smaller and loose items are placed on a tray or in a small box to keep them safe. Following the instructions, remove the first parts to be assembled from their sprue or retainer. Carefully cut away the item from the moulding sprue with the aid of the craft knife or a special sprue cutting tool, then clean away any moulding remaining using a needle file or glass paper wrapped around a small flat square of timber. When cutting brass etching away from its retainer by using a knife, use a flat piece of hardwood or other hard surface underneath on which to push and cut down through the securing brass tabs. Do not use a cutting mat for cutting brass etchings as it has a soft surface and will allow the etch to bend under the cutting knife's downward pressure. An alternative with brass etching is to use a fine, small pair of scissors – a sharp pair of nail scissors is the best option here. However, I have found it best to use special sprue cutters!

If the kit is a plastic building, normally the first two major pieces to be joined are walls – the end wall and one longer front or rear wall. It may be easier to fit doors and windows before proceeding further. Place the two walls together, as a dry fit, on the glass sheet. If you are satisfied that they are correct, hold them together by applying a small strip of masking tape around the outside on the two pieces. This will temporarily hold them in place, allowing you to open the bottle of solvent (in its mug!) and dip the artist's brush into it. Apply the brush to the inside of the corner join and run it up and down the seam. The solvent will be drawn into the joint by capillary action. Check and ensure that the two surfaces are still correctly in line, then take the engineer's square and check that the two walls are at the correct 90-degree angle (assuming that is what the angle of the joint should be). Carefully place the bonded surfaces to one side to allow the bond to cure, ideally overnight, and make sure the joint is still at the correct angle.

Proceed with the construction of the opposite pair of walls, and again leave them overnight to set. Once set, remove the masking tape. The two cured wall sections can now be bonded together to form the basic 'box' shape of the building. Use the glass sheet to ensure that the walls are level along their bottom edges and apply strips of masking tape to each corner before gluing. Check all is square and, once satisfied, apply the solvent to the inner edges of the two joints using the artist's brush. Again, ideally allow the solvent to cure overnight. Remove the tape and a solid box shape should be the result.

Remember, when test dry assembling the components together before gluing, any irregularities preventing a close fit of the two items can be gently removed with a flat needle file or fine glass paper wrapped around, for example, a solid piece of wood.

Where card kits are to be constructed I use either neat PVA wood-working adhesive or a special card bonding glue such as Roket. The PVA is applied with a small artist's-style brush or, in very small areas, with the tip of a cocktail stick.

Once the building has been constructed and painted as necessary, it needs to be brought to life. Super-detailing areas around the building will vastly improve its appearance and make it that little bit different from all the other similar models produced from the same kit. The following detailing can be carried out on all types of buildings – card, plastic or resin, etc.

Always ensure that the building sits *into* its surroundings and does not sit on top of the land or area, as a visible building-to-land joint line is unsightly and unrealistic. Place the building into its final location, then add the surroundings – earth, pavements, road surface, concrete, etc – up to the wall of the building. If your building needs to be removable, consider making a small sub-base onto which the building is bonded, the sub-base being larger than the building. The joints between the main layout landscape and the sub-base can be disguised by walls, paving, fencing, hedges, etc – in fact, anything that would normally be found around the outer area of the building.

Adding creeper growth to the sides of some buildings will make them look more part of the landscape. Grass tufts, flowers or any rough undergrowth can help disguise the buildings-to-landscape interface, especially with older or more derelict and unkempt buildings.

Look carefully at real-life buildings, and note the way in which they seem normally to blend into their setting. Exceptions will be found, and many newly constructed buildings can look out of place until their surroundings mature. This 'new-build' look can be modelled and can often form a focal point of a small cameo setting. Add sections of soil pipes, timber, bricks, piles of earth, etc, all of which are all found on new-build sites, together with scaffolding and ladders, of course. Mechanical diggers and mobile compressors for pneumatic drills are also found on modern building sites. A 'hole in the earth' (a baseboard hole) where pipes or cables can be seen with a workman digging will also add to the illusion of realism. Almost all the items needed for adding super-detailing to a building or its surrounding can be purchased ready made or made by the modeller using odd items from the scrap box. An example is pipes, which can be produced by cutting up lengths of plastic tubing. Cables laid on the ground or air pipes for pneumatic drills, etc, can be produced from fine electrical wire or the insulation stripped from small wires.

Ground cover can be produced using several materials. A hanging basket liner is

This church scene is enhanced by details such as the wedding party, photographer, gravestones, etc. Adding illumination inside the church is effective, especially if stained glass window representations are used.

one such, and can be used to represent grass on larger areas. Glue it with PVA to the sub-base structure then, once the glue has fully dried, the liner is pulled off the sub-base, leaving behind tufts or hairs of the liner which, once touched in with suitably coloured paint, represent undergrowth. Scenic mat can be glued over a pre-shaped former. Flocks and scatters, sold by model shops or war game stores, are used to represent grass and earth, etc – they are simply sprinkled onto a coating of neat PVA glue either onto previously painted areas or onto the scenic mat. Static grass can be used to produce grass and weeds that are able to stand up from the surface to which they are glued; they are applied onto neat PVA glue using either an electric static grass application tool or a puffer bottle. Both produce strands of grass that stand upright in the PVA and, once the glue has dried, they can, if need be, be trimmed with small scissors to the height required. Adding spots of neat PVA glue to the tops of some static grass tufts, then sprinkling on lighter shades of ground cover material or scatters of a completely different colour, can add to the illusion of weeds, flowers and other undergrowth.

We are no longer limited to producing kits from ready-produced parts sold in a box or packet. There are now downloadable construction kits available from the internet. You normally buy the download, though some are free, and once it has been downloaded and saved to your PC you then print off as many copies as you need, or a part of an item to enhance or alter other buildings. There is no limit to the number of times the item can be printed. These are all card and printed paper constructions, and during and after construction it is well worthwhile to spray the freshly printed papers once the ink has dried and before they are cut up into individual parts or glued onto the card backing; use an artist's matt varnish from an aerosol can, or if you have an air brush use artist's matt varnish diluted by 50% with IPA (Isopropanol Alcohol). This seals the printer ink and paper from any moisture in the glue being used to construct the item. Also, overspray the whole completed structure once the final building work has finished and it has fully dried; this will prevent moisture in the air causing damage to the printed papers and card surfaces. Cover any glazed windows with cut strips of repositionable note-type pre-glued paper, which will act as a mask to prevent the varnish being applied to the window glazing during the spraying process' peel off the strips once the varnish has dried.

On plastic, metal and laser-cut wooden models the use of fine-finish modelling putty is highly recommended for infilling any gaps or visible joins in the completed and painted model. By spraying the area with a light coat of car primer paint or a similar primer paint that is suitable for models, the application can quickly reveal misaligned parts or other areas that require the application of the modelling putty to correct bad joints, etc. Work the soft putty into the gaps and uneven areas, leave to set, then scrape, sand or file off the surplus until a correct profile is obtained. Overspray lightly with the primer again to double-check that the repair or correction is now good.

7
Point control

To operate a layout's points there are several methods available.

Manually by finger: This is OK but isn't ideal where points are located remotely from the operation position, or are just not easily reached.

Wire in tube or rod: Solid rods can be used both above or below the baseboard. Flexible wire or a flexible nylon rod is threaded inside a protective tube and by push/pull operation of the wire or rod the point is moved over and back. The operation can be from mechanical-signalling-type levers or by basic push/pull rods emerging from the side frame of the baseboard with little more than a cork or wooden round ball on the end. The same can be used for solid rod operation, but here right-angled cranks are used to transfer movement around any corners or right-angles.

Point rodding: There are at least two and possibly more manufacturers of prototypical mechanical point rodding – actual working rodding, not just visual. The rod run starts from a point lever and runs out along the trackside and, via 'L'-shaped cranks, turns through 90 degrees as required to cross the track before fitting onto the point stretcher bar (tie bar) which moves the points over and back. Installing large amounts of this is a demanding task and it is certainly is not suitable for layouts that are portable and have baseboards jointed together. But both visually and operationally it is very impressive.

Electrically by solenoid: This has been used for many years and is still the most popular means of moving the point blades. Two coils of wire are formed and inside the coils a metal iron core is free to move between them. A drive pin is fitted onto the iron core, passing the core's movement to the points' stretcher or tie bar. Applying power to one coil momentarily energises it and causes a magnetic field to be produced, which pulls the iron core into the energised coil's centre. Energising the opposite coil pulls the iron core into that coil's centre. It is very important that the coil is only energised momentarily, normally for no longer than half a second. If the power is left on for too long there is a great risk of the coil burning out, rendering the motor defective. Thus the normal means of switching the power to the coils are: passing contact levers; non-locking sprung-to-centre-off toggle switches; press-to-make non-locking push buttons; or a stud and probe. DCC accessory point decoders can also be used to operate solenoid point motors. Solenoids work on either AC or DC power, and normally their operating voltage is between 12 and 20 volts, but they do draw a considerable current when operated, typically around 3 amps instantaneously.

Electrically by an electric motor: These are often called 'slow motion' or 'stall' motors, although some are not of the stall type. Both types use a small electric motor and gearing to slowly move a drive pin from one end of the motor's body to the other, the pin being connected to the points' stretcher or tie bar. Normally the points' over-centre spring fitted to most ready-made points is removed to allow the motor to reproduce a more realistic slow-motion drive of the points' switch blades. Unlike solenoids, these motors do not use passing contact levers or switches; instead, they require the operating power to be left on even when they have finished their travel. Stall types, via their internal circuitry, put the motor into a stalled condition at the end of its travel, with low-current power continually being applied to the motor. The non-stall types drive to the end of their travel and, via internal contacts, cut off the operating power; the drive remains in the end position of travel locked by the gearing, preventing further free movement.

To make either type of motor drive to the opposite end, the power feed is reversed, causing the motor to drive to the other end of its travel and again stall or be disconnected and remain in position. These motors usually operate on DC power, though half-wave rectified AC can also be used. Some will work on AC power too. They draw a very small current when running, and normally even less when the stall type is stalled; of course, the non-stall type has a zero-power consumption when stopped at the end of its travel. Typical running current is between 15 and 35 milliamps (0.015 to 0.035A) and 5 to 15 milliamps when stalled. The operating voltage varies with make, but can be between 7 to 20 volts. Manufacturers include Tortoise and Cobalt, with Conrad producing an AC operating motor. As usual there are other manufacturers.

Electrically by a servo: Servos were predominately the preserve of the radio-control modeller – planes, boats and cars, etc. Simply put, the servo is an electric motor controlled by a series of power pulses. The length and frequency of the pulse determines the movement of the motor. Normally a servo turns a maximum of 90 degrees left or right of its neutral position (180 degrees overall) – these are positional rotation servos, and their movement can be controlled to be less than 90 degrees each way. They require external electronic circuitry to provide the operating pulses. They do occasionally suffer from what is known as 'servo twitch' or 'buzzing', which is often caused by having the control wiring too long or running too close to interference sources, or the servo is being driven too hard against the stop position. Keep the control cables as short as possible and try not to exceed a 2-metre length, as beyond that you risk the possibility of interference and possible volt drop. Advancements in servo design and their operating circuitry are making them more cost effective for the model railway user. Servos can be analogue or digital styles, but digital servos tend to draw more current. Servos operate at around 4.5 to 6 volts. Ideally for railway modelling use, consider analogue servos for operating points and digital servos for items that need finer control, such as semaphore signal arms. One thing to remember with servos is the sheer number that may be in use; when larger numbers are involved there is a need for large power current requirements involving the use of multiple power supplies, or a larger-current single power supply, especially where multi-output servo control boards are used.

Which switch?

Which switches are used for electrical operation of the point motors? This depends on the type of motor. As previously stated, solenoid motors must only have a brief momentary pulse of power applied to the coil, so it is vital that the power is removed quickly. This is achieved by using passing contact levers. As the lever is moved from one end to the other, contacts inside it make then break the connection to the motor coil, thereby providing the momentary pulse needed. Levers tend to be costly, so the canny modeller will look for suitable alternatives! These are mainly (On)-Off-(On) toggle switches, where the bracketed (On) cannot remain in that position when the switch's toggle lever is released. These switches are under sprung tension and return to the centre Off position from either end of its travel. Toggle switches are often used in control panels where banks of switches are positioned to operate the points, or they are placed on the mimic track plan where the point they are to operate is drawn. These switches are of the Single Pole Double Throw (SPDT) type of non-locking sprung-to-centre-off style for solenoids.

Next is the push-to-make non-locking press button. Two of these are needed for each motor, one for each feed to the coil. When pressed they apply power to the coil and once released the switch returns to the off position.

Finally comes 'stud and probe' operation. This system is normally used with a mimic control panel where a simple representation of the actual layout track is reproduced, with the points shown. Two studs are fitted into the panel's board for each set of points, and by applying the probe momentarily to the appropriate stud, power is sent to the motor's coil.

For slow motion (stall and non-stall) switches. conventionally locking On-On switches are used. Slow motion motors need to have the power polarity reversible, allowing allow the motor to move one way under one polarity, then in the opposite direction by reversing the polarity. For DC operation of slow motion motors, a Double Pole Double Throw (DPDT) switch is used.

Servos normally use a locking On-Off Single Pole Single Throw (SPST) or Single Pole Double Throw (SPDT) switch. Double Throw switches can be used instead of Single Throw types and are at times more readily available. One end tab and the middle tab are used for single throw operation; the remaining tab at the other end of the switch is not used.

Solenoid point motors have fairly low resistance coils, typically 3 to 5 ohms. This means that the current flowing in the coil at our applied voltage is fairly high, but it is only a momentary pulse. Ohm's law comes into play here, so if our supply volts are DC and at 15 volts and the coil is 4 ohms, the current flow is 3.75 amps. AC will be a little higher! While this power is momentary, it needs to be considered when designing your circuit, allowing the correct wire sizing to be used.

You may wish to operate signals or have indication lights relating to the points' position. Therefore you will need some form of point- or point-motor-operated change-over switch. Some point motors allow an optional extra switch to be bonded onto the motor and as the motor moves over and back the switch changes too. A typical example is the Peco PL10 motor fitted with the SPDT Peco PL13 switch or the DPDT Peco PL15 micro-switch; via the switch's contacts accessories are fed from a separate power source or the switch is used to feed live-frog point frogs. Seep PM1 and the self-locking PM4 have a built-in SPDT switch that can be used to switch accessories or provide the power to a live frog point frog.

Tortoise and some Cobalt motors usually have a minimum of two separate change-over contacts fitted internally, so there are two SPDT switches provided. Some Cobalts have an output that is for frog polarity or LED indication operation, but this is internally wired to the drive input power for the motor and provides a low-current supply to external devices, these are fitted to the Cobalt iP motor range.

If you use surface-mounted solenoid motors like the Peco PL11, Hornby R8243 or Gaugemaster PM20, currently there are no means of fitting an accessory switch directly to them. You therefore have two choices. One is to use a micro-switch fitted to the opposite side of the point, with its lever worked by the points' moving stretcher or tie bar. If this is visually unacceptable, I recommend the use of a *twin coil* unlatch relay; note the emphasis on 'twin coil', which is wired to the motor's three operation wires and is mechanically latched in one position by one relay coil being energised momentarily as the point motor receives a pulse of power to operate it. The mechanical latch is released by the point motor coil for the other direction, receiving a pulse to the point motor coil and the other latching relay's coil and being momentarily energised. Only a pulse is needed to latch and unlatch the coils of the relay, so it is ideal for use with solenoid motors. The relay coil requires a DC power source to work, so the point motors should ideally be fed from a DC supply or from the output of a CDU (Capacitor Discharge Unit), which is DC even if the input to the CDU is AC. However, by adding diodes to the feed paths to the relay coils, these latching relays work happily on AC power feeds to the point motor. By means of the latching relay's contacts, accessories are switched and fed.

Most twin-coil latching relays have two separate change-over contacts DPDT; one contact set can be used for live frog switching, or both used for other applications such as point position panel indications or signalling controls, etc. The relays have fine connection pins and are ideally plugged into an Integrated Circuit Dual In Line (IC DIL) socket with the number of pins to accommodate the relay's pins; alternatively the relays can be directly soldered to suitable PCB (Printed Circuit Board) tracks. Where a DIL socket or direct relay fitting is used, it is soldered to a circuit board – copper-tracked stripboard being ideal – and the wires are soldered to the board's copper strips. Don't forget to gap the copper tracks between adjacent pins! These simple relay sets can be pre-made on the workbench, then fitted to the layout. Ready-made latching relay units are also available.

The unit all made up on a piece of stripboard ready to be fitted to the layout's point motor wiring. The two rows of three terminals top and bottom are the relay contacts, while on the left are the connection terminals to the motor wiring.

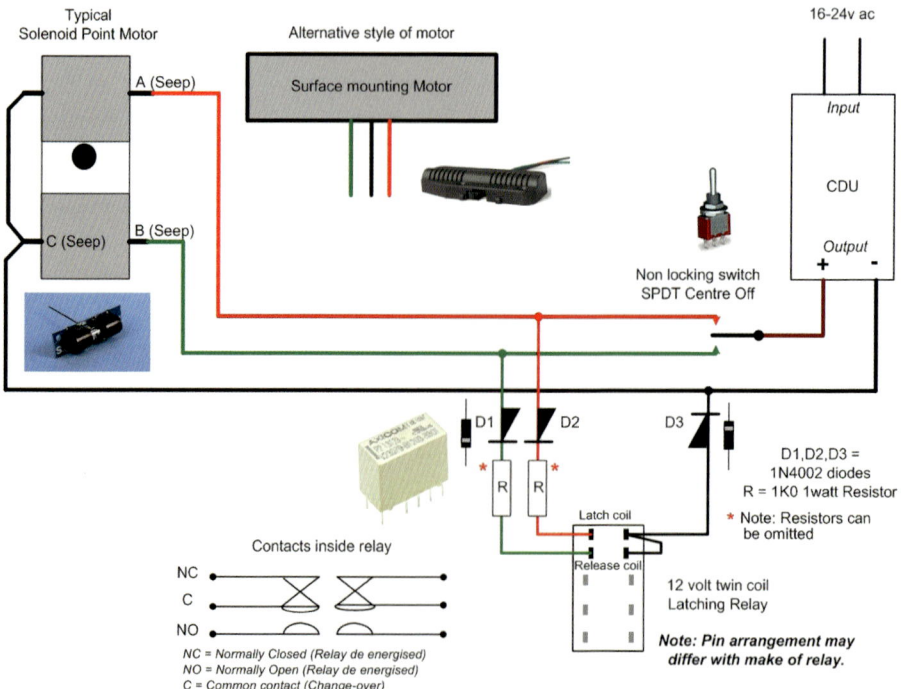

The simple wiring of a twin-coil latching relay wired to the three operation wires running to a solenoid point motor. This is for conventional (analogue) point control. For the DCC user, the circuit is slightly different, and is shown later in the DCC section. Do not try and use the circuit shown here with a DCC accessory decoder.

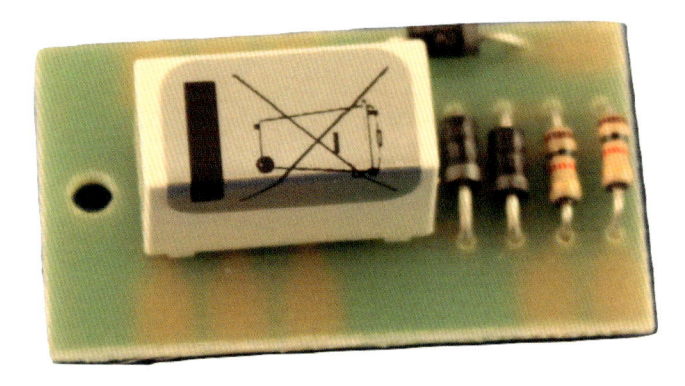

An example of a ready-made latching relay unit. This particular one is the GM500 by Gaugemaster, seen in comparison to the size of a 20 pence piece.

A CDU (Capacitor Discharge Unit) provides the solenoid point motor with a 'beefy' pulse of power. The pulse is pre-stored in the capacitor and is released as soon as the point lever or switch is operated. Normally only one CDU is needed for the whole layout, although very large layouts with multiple operating areas may well require a second or third CDU. The CDU not only provides the heavy-duty pulse of power to the point motor coil, but also helps stop accidental solenoid coil burn-out occurring, should a point switch accidently remain on for too long, as the CDU cannot recharge until all the point switches are back in their off position. Only a few milliamps flow through the point motor coil in the event of a switch remaining on after the initial discharge has occurred. A CDU is installed after the point motor power source and before the first switch or lever. Note that a CDU does not work very well with the existing Hornby R044 black point lever, due to the lever's internal switching arrangements, but one does work well with all other passing contact levers and switches. CDUs work best with a 16-volt AC input; this is converted to DC via on-board diodes and they always give a DC output. You can feed the CDU with DC power, but this is then best increased to around 19 to 22 volts DC. Always check that your CDU can operate at this voltage and, if visible, that the capacitor is rated at 25 volts or higher. Most should be!

Three Capacitor Discharge Units (CDUs). That on the left has four capacitors and gives a heavy-duty output, ideal for use where a diode matrix is used to move several points at once from one switch. The middle CDU has twin capacitors fitted and is ideal for medium-sized layouts, while the right-hand example has one capacitor and will happily work one or more solenoid motors at once. *Images courtesy of BLOCKsignalling*

8
Digital Command Control (DCC)

As mentioned in an earlier chapter, DCC is the newer control method and is becoming increasingly popular. It will probably never replace DC, as many modellers prefer to use DC control, but DCC has gained many supporters and often those taking up the hobby afresh will opt to go down the DCC route from the beginning.

So what is so special about DCC? It enables you to control up to 9,999 locomotives all on one layout (if you can get that many on one layout!), each sharing the same power and rails as all the others; to move one loco while next to it another loco remains stationary; to turn on or off lighting on locos or inside carriages; and to have sounds playing that are recordings taken from the real locomotives represented on the model, following what the model loco does so that the exhaust rate increases as a steam loco pulls away or the engine revs build up on a diesel loco.

Notice that I mentioned 9,999. This is the conventional range of address numbers used by most DCC systems, starting at 1 and going through to 9999 (note that some basic DCC control systems do not allow the full range of address numbers to be used and only offer 1 to 9 or 1 to 59 or similarly low digit address numbers). You, as the end user, set the unique address number for each item (decoder) that you have connected to your DCC system. Once set, the decoder remembers this address number until you change it. For example, taking a loco with address number 10 to another DCC-operated layout, it will still only respond to a command when address number 10 is sent to it on the other system. If you have two or more items with the same address number, they will all do whatever you request when that address number is sent out by the system. For example, two locomotives given the same address number will both move off together in the same direction and at the same speed. Speed is also governed by other external factors such as gearing and friction, so no two locomotives will ever perform exactly the same. Running trains with more than one locomotive is called 'double heading' in the UK or a 'consist' in the US.

All mobile decoders (loco decoders) are supplied new with a default address of 3, and the purchaser should change this address number to whatever is required. Keeping the decoder at 3 can lead to minor problems, especially when other new locos are obtained and have the same address number. I therefore always recommend changing it. Many operators use all or some of the digits of the loco's actual running number.

DCC allows for two ranges of address numbers, 'short address' and 'long address'. Short address, or two digit addressing, is in the range 1 to 127. I can hear you now saying '127' – that's three digits! DCC uses the binary coding system and numbers from 1 to 127 are classed as being in the two-digit range. Long address or four-digit addressing is in the 1 to 9999 range. Technically four-digit address numbering can go to 10238, but the vast majority of control systems stop at 9999. It should also be noted that some DCC systems use 1 to 99 and 10 to 9999, while others can use

1 to 127 and have four-digit addresses starting at 128! There is no defined method, so read your DCC systems manual!

If you have up to 20 or 30 locos, consider two-digit addressing. Some makes of DCC control systems and some mobile decoders do not accept four-digit addressing, though mobile decoders that are restricted to two-digit addressing are now quite rare! But some can still be found, so be cautious if you specifically want four-digit addressing.

You can technically have 9,999 locos all sitting on your tracks with only one moving! In reality this isn't going to happen, but the option is there if ever needed. Note that address 0 (Zero) is reserved on some DCC systems to enable one DC locomotive without a decoder fitted to be operated by the DCC command unit; however, not every DCC system allows this, and it does come with a serious word of caution: allowing a DC loco without a decoder fitted to remain on DCC-powered rails while stationary risks the loco's motor being burned out very quickly. This is due to the high-frequency DCC arriving at the motor and causing the motor's armature and coils to rapidly swap polarity, with the result that the armature starts to hunt back and forth microscopically. This will cause the motor's coil windings to eventually overheat; there is even a risk of them getting so hot that they eventually burn out! So be warned, and if at all possible avoid using a DC loco on DCC, even under address number 0. Always fit a decoder and no harm will then come to the loco. Normally a DCC-fitted loco can be used on DC systems as long as DC operation hasn't been disabled.

DCC provides a constant voltage to the rails all of the time, so unlike DC, where the rail volts vary, DCC is always on and ideally fed to all parts of the railway. Self-isolation of points should be overcome to allow unset routes to be powered even when the point is set to the opposite direction. Rail volts are typically in the range of 12 to 16 and are a sort of AC not DC! The AC used is not of the conventional sine wave format like mains power – 50Hz in the UK . DCC tends to be in the 8,000Hz to 10,000KHz range (8KHz-10KHz) or around that frequency. Its wave form is more akin to being bipolar or square wave, but neither of those terminologies are 100% correct. To accurately read DCC rail volts you need a multimeter that can read True RMS voltage at 10KHz. A standard domestic multimeter set to its AC voltage range can be used, but the reading shown will not be accurate; however, it is a good indication and should be the same all around the layout. The other accurate measuring means are to use a ramp meter, which is specifically made to measure DCC voltage, or an oscilloscope.

Once the decoder receives it package of data and the data has arrived correctly, the decoder will perform whatever instruction is contained in that package. This might, for example, be 'stop', 'move forwards at half speed', 'change direction of travel', or 'turn on lighting or sounds'. Once the instruction has been acted upon, the decoder continues to do it until it is told to do something else. I used the postman analogy earlier; this is about the simplest description, and is repeated here in case you missed it… Think of DCC instructions or packets of data as being like a postman delivering a letter with instructions in it. The postman only puts the letter through the letterbox of No 38, and the occupant of No 38 reads the instruction and acts upon it. All the other house numbers from 1 to 9,999 have seen the postman on his round, but haven't received the letter, so they carry on doing what they were last doing!

There are two main types of DCC decoder: mobile decoders designed to fit inside locomotives, etc, and static decoders known as accessory decoders. The latter are stationary and operate devices like point motors and signals, or simply turn lineside lighting on or off, etc.

Mobile decoders come in three styles.

Function only These have no motor control circuitry and are normally fitted into carriages or the rear unpowered carriages of diesel multiple units (DMUs) or electric multiple units (EMUs) to provide rear directional lighting and internal lighting, etc.

Motor control with additional function outputs These offer full motor control but additionally have function outputs that are used to feed and control other loco devices such as front and rear directional lighting, firebox fire flicker, smoke generator and cab lighting, etc. These additional outputs are called 'functions', and are switched on or off by the DCC system's 'F' keys. Decoders can have one function output or many; currently ten is about the maximum. Mainstream mid-price decoders will normally offer three or four function outputs.

Sound decoders These are normally manufactured as combined sound, motor and function output all in the one package, although sound-only decoders are available. Basically, they are the same as motor decoders but are frequently larger in size and may well have two wires provided to connect to a suitable ohm loudspeaker. Four function outputs are common, but some makes offer six and even ten function outputs.

Decoder outputs (functions), as previously stated, are used to operate lights or other features fitted into the locomotive. All decoders with wiring harnesses use a common wiring colour coding, as shown below. A decoder's function output is nominally at 12 volts DC and is switched on the negative function wires. Common to all the functions, the blue wire is used to feed positive DC to all features connected to the function wires; all other function wires are switched negatives. The actual DC voltage on the function output will depend on the DCC rail volts minus about 2 volts; hence DCC rail volts of 14 volts will proved around 12 volts DC on the function outputs.

The current standard for mobile decoder wires is:

Red to right-hand-side wheel
Black to left-hand-side wheel
Orange to motor terminal 'A'
Grey to other motor terminal 'B'
Blue is common positive to all functions
White is normally reserved for forward (white) lights
Yellow is normally reserved for rear (red) lights
Green is frequently cab lighting control but can be used for any other feature
Violet or purple is used as required, for firebox flicker, other lighting or to feed a smoke generator

The most commonly used function outputs are the two direction-of-travel outputs, which on wired decoders are found on the white and yellow wires. These are normally turned on and off by the command station's F0 key. They will automatically swap power between the white and yellow wires when the direction of travel button is operated. For forward moves the white wire is on, and when the loco is travelling in reverse the yellow wire is on, both in relation to the common positive blue wire.

Additional function outputs are typically a green wire operated on non-sound decoders by the F1 key. and the purple or violet wire operated by the F2 key. Note that some decoders will use different F key numbers and sound decoders will always be different. Refer to the decoder manual or leaflet to determine which function output is controlled by which F key.

At this stage it should be mentioned that there are other connection styles of decoders, mainly 6 pin, 8 pin and 21 pin. 6- and 21-pin decoders plug directly into special sockets in the loco and normally do not have any wires attached. All the connections are carried through the pins onto the loco's printed circuit board where they are distributed as required around the circuit board and finally off to the item they are needed to power.

Another style of mobile decoder is called PluX and was originally intended to replace all UK 6-, 8- and 21-pin decoder connections, but for whatever reason so far the main UK train manufactures have not adopted this standard. They may well do so in the future, so here are the PluX details. PluX has been designed to be available in 22-, 16- and 8-pin configuration, the latter two being able to directly plug into a 22 PluX socket. A 12-pin version has also been mooted but hasn't appeared on the NMRA listing as yet (NMRA is the National Model Railroad Association in North America, which sets standards for DCC and other model railway features, offering a common ground approach for manufacturers to follow).

Just to add confusion, a further style of mobile decoder called NEXT18 is being considered for use by some manufacturers. This is an 18-pin direct plug-in decoder. It is therefore very wise to double check when purchasing a DCC-ready loco to find out what type and style of DCC socket it has been fitted with.

When a DCC loco is placed on the track, assuming forward direction is selected on the command station, the loco will move forwards. If it is removed from the track, turned through 180 degrees and returned to the DCC power rails it will still move in the forward direction, unlike a DC loco, which will run in the opposite direction when turned through 180 degrees. This is easy to relate to if using a steam locomotive, as the chimney is normally at the front, but what about diesel-outline models? In the UK the No 1 end is conventionally the end with the fan in the roof, but it is always worth double-checking the real locomotive, pictures and its build details.

There are basically three types of model locomotives that the DCC user needs to be aware of:

DCC-fitted or DCC on board: These all come with a decoder prefitted by the manufacturer or in some cases by the retailer.

DCC-ready: This as sold is a DC-only locomotive. It has inside a special socket fitted to enable a DCC decoder to be plugged in, but as sold the socket is occupied by a DC-operation-only plug. To convert to DCC, open the loco, or its tender, ease out the DC plug from the socket and remove it, keeping it safe as you may want to revert back to DC-only operation should you ever sell the loco or wish to test it on DC power. Plug in a DCC decoder of a suitable choice and size, ensuring that the decoder's plug, or the decoder itself for direct-pin-fitting versions, is installed the correct way around.

Non-DCC-ready: These will mainly be older pre-DCC-era locomotives and will require some rewiring and electrical testing to ensure that the wheels and metal chassis are not making contact with either of the two motor connections before the decoder's wires are soldered in. Decoders use red wire to the right-hand wheel pick-ups, and black wire to the left-hand wheel pick-ups, with orange and grey wires to the motor connections. On no account must the red and black wires or their connection places make connection with the orange and grey wires. Once converted, test the loco on the programming track, then, assuming all is correct, place the loco onto the main DCC-powered tracks and test it. If it runs the opposite way to the console's direction setting, either reverse the orange and grey wires on the motor or, if you wish change the value of CV29, increase it by 1 if the existing value is an even number, or reduce it by 1 if it is currently an odd number. e.g. read 6 make it 7, or read 7 then make it 6.

What is CV (Configuration Variable)? Put simply it is like specific 'tuning slots' that, when adjusted by altering the decimal number in the CV's value, it alters how the decoder will perform a specific task assigned to that CV. Think of a CV as being like a radio station setting. You tune the radio to receive the station, then fine tune it more to make the station clearer. The CV is the radio station and the value is the fine tuning. The easiest to understand is CV1, which is the address number of the decoder. By adjusting the value of CV1 the loco's address number is changed. Below is a list of the most common CVs and what they adjust. It must be noted that while the CVs shown below are the basic ones, there can be many hundreds of them in advanced decoders and not all makes of decoder are allocated the same CV numbers for the same

CV No.	Description
1	Decoder Address. Default setting is normally 3
2	Start Voltage
3	Acceleration rate
4	Deceleration rate
5	Max (top) speed
6	Speed Curve Modifier
7	Manufactures version number
8	Manufactures ID number/ Decoder reset

features, though these basic ones are all common.

Static or non-mobile accessory decoders offer the DCC user an interface to allow the operation by DCC of all other accessories, such as point motors, signalling and anything else power-operated on the layout. These are normally referred to as accessory decoders, or point decoders if they only operate point motors. They all take data from the DCC system and provide one or more switched outputs. Some use the DCC as a power source, while others allow connection to a separate power supply to feed the item(s) connected to the decoder. Typically accessory decoders come in single, twin, four, six or eight outputs per decoder. Some have fixed outputs that are pulse only for operating solenoid motors, such as the DCC Concepts ADS-2sx or ADS-8sx decoders, while other styles can have their outputs set between pulse or continuous – Hornby's R8247 and the ESU SwitchPilot are two examples. A pulse output is used for solenoid motors while a continuous output is used to power colour light signals, lighting, or stall point motors. A third type is the continuous-output-only decoder. Mostly these are designed to work with stall point motors. One such is the DCC Concepts AD-2fx – note that the 'S' is missing from this part number compared to the earlier one referred to, as this decoder is not suitable for solenoid motors, only stall motors.

Accessory decoders that offer a pulse output will have three connections per output. Most will use the markings '+' 'C' and '-', while others will use 'L', 'C' and 'R' for Left, Common and Right. The C is the common connection and is positive to the switched '+' and '-' or 'L' and 'R' connections, which are both negative regardless of being marked '+'! A conventional solenoid point motor will connect to the three terminals of the one output. An example is the Seep PM1 connecting its pad A to '+', pad B to '-' and pad C to 'C'. Decoders designed solely for continuous output may have either three or just two terminals per output depending on the make. Examples of two terminals per output are the DCC Concepts AD1 or AD4 decoders, which are designed to operate an

A typical accessory decoder suitable for solenoid point motor operation only. *Courtesy of DCC Concepts*

An alternative accessory point decoder produced by Train-Tech. This is for use with solenoid-style point motors.

analogue Cobalt point motor per output. The AD1 version offers just one output while the AD4 gives four separate outputs to operate four analogue Cobalt motors.

As mentioned in the DC (analogue) section, if your point motor doesn't have any change-over contacts fitted, e.g. Peco PL11, Hornby R8243 or Gaugemaster PM20, etc, the use of a twin-coil latching relay can be used to provide a dual set of change-over contacts. The one shown in the DC section is not suitable for use with an accessory decoder, as the decoder switches the two negative outputs often referenced on the accessory decoders output terminals as '+' and '-', while the 'C'

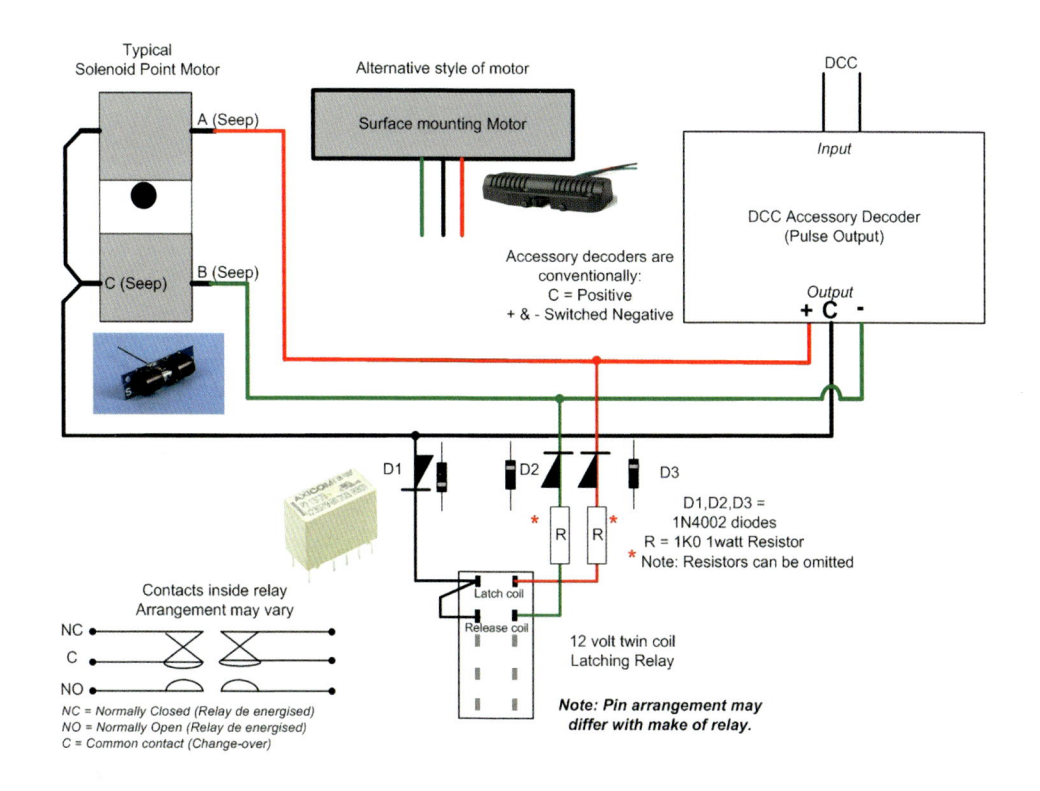

A revised circuit for use with a pulse output DCC accessory decoder.

connection is positive to both of the other two – see the accompanying drawing.

On our DCC layout there are a few other items that will not normally be found on the DC layout. One such is the Reverse Loop Module (RLM). As the name suggests this is used on a single-line reverse loop of track or a 'Y' point track configuration. A reverse loop is where the left-hand rail at one end of the loop becomes the right-hand rail at the other end, and thereby meets a rail that is at the opposite polarity. If left without some form of action, this will result in a full short circuit occurring. Initially the entrance and exit places of the loop are electrically separated from the main lines by inserting Insulated Rail Joiners (IRJs) into both rails opposite each other at both locations, leaving the loop's rails totally isolated from the rest of the railway, and only fed from the output of the RLM. The RLM is designed to detect a short circuit, and instantly swaps over its output pair of connections. So, our train entering a reverse loop finds that the loop's rails are at the same polarity and carries on as normal; however, as it exits the loop the main-line rails are at opposite polarity, which produces a momentary short circuit as the loco's metal wheels bridge the exit IRJs. The RLM detects the short and flips the reverse loop's rails polarity over before the main console detects the short occurring. This of course removes the shorting problem, and all happens in microseconds. Now the loop's rails are at opposite polarity at the entrance IRJs! When another train enters the loop from the main-line end and its metal wheels bridge the entrance IRJs, the RLM again detects the short and instantly flips over the loop rails polarity to match that of the incoming rails. The short circuit is thus removed and the train carries on as though nothing has occurred, then as it exits the loop the rails will be out of phase again with the main line and the RLM flips the loop rails back to match the exit track's polarity.

One thing to remember with a reverse loop is that the entrance and exit IRJs need to be further apart than the longest train to travel over the loop section, i.e. the whole train, loco, wagons or carriages, should all fit in between the entrance and exit pairs of IRJs. The size of the loop can easily be increased by moving one or both IRJs further out along the main line. The reason this is important is we do not want the metal wheels of our rolling stock to be able to cause the RLM to flip should the loco be exiting while the rear is still travelling over the entrance IRJs. The RLM will be continually flipping over its output polarity and eventually the main console will detect the shorting and cause the entire system to shut down – not a helpful situation! Thus the reverse loop between the IRJs needs to be longer then the longest ever train to travel over that loop.

There are some 'work-arounds' to prevent this. Having all rolling stock fitted with plastic wheels is one. This is not a recommended procedure, as plastic wheels are renowned for collecting and spreading rail-generated 'muck' and cause more poor running problems than they are worth. I highly recommend not fitting plastic wheel sets! Alternatively the rails at the entrance and exit to the loops can be isolated for a few millimetres by fitting additional IRJs or cutting through the rails and inserting an insulating material into the gap, then profiling it to the rail shape. This insulating material – plastic normally or an epoxy resin allowed to set, then shaped to the rail profile – prevents the rails touching each other, especially when the air temperature increases, and rails expand a little. The idea is that the insulated gap stops the metal wheels of a carriage or wagon being able to bridge the main-line rails to the loop's rails by the insulated rail, which is only a couple or so millimetres in length. The major down side of this option is that any rolling stock with interconnected wheel sets (carriages with lighting, where multi-wheel pick-up is used, or metal bogies on wagons or carriages, etc) will still cause the RLM to continually flip, as too will a loco with a long wheelbase, so while it works generally it is not foolproof and

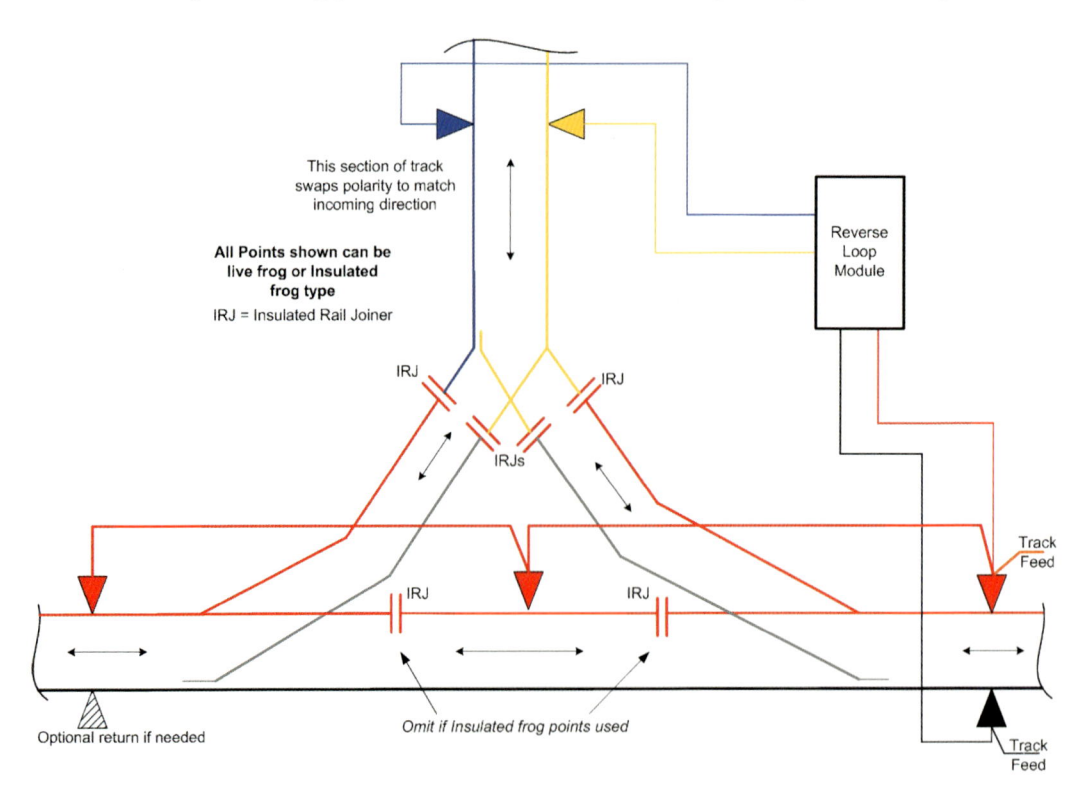

A typical DCC reverse loop module feed for a triangle track arrangement.

can still lead to problems. Therefore really it is best to ensure that the actual length of the loop between IRJs is always longer than the longest complete train to travel over the loop.

Our RLM can also be used on some makes of turntable where a continuous feed to the rotating bridge rails is provided.

Another option for reverse loop control on DCC is to use a Frog Juicer with two outputs (Dual Juicer). These two outputs feed the loop's rails and flip the loop's polarity as required. Again the loop should be longer than the longest train to use it.

Some DCC (and DC for that matter) users will employ a Double Pole Double Throw (DPDT) switch, often fitted to the points that control entrance to and exit from the reverse loop. By means of the DPDT switch's contacts, the loop rail polarity is changed over with the movement of the point itself.

The next item found on DCC layouts but not on DC ones is the Booster. This device provides a secondary source of power output that is often greater than that from the main DCC console, or is used to feed a totally separate section of track that is isolated from the main-line feed from the main DCC console.

The Booster can be used (depending on make) to increase the current (amperes) available from a standard DCC system or to feed a totally isolated separate area of the layout. Here all rails leading into and out of the Booster-controlled section are insulated from all other areas by fitting Insulated Rail Joiners (IRJs) to all rails.

Some Boosters, but not all, can take DCC commands directly from the rails or the DCC bus pair of wires fed from the main command station, but many have to use a dedicated output socket on the command station via a dedicated data cable that connects command station to Booster; again this is type dependant. Boosters will have their own power supplies to feed them and to provide the output to the Booster-fed rails. A Booster will have its own internal overload protection, which will cut off its output to the rails in the event of a short circuit, but will still leave the main command station operating correctly.

Asymmetric Brake Control (ABC Braking)

ABC is used for fully automatic non-computer-controlled stopping at and pulling away from certain places such as signals or platforms or wherever an automatic stop is required. ABC can be employed anywhere so long as the loco decoder supports it. Note that not all decoders support ABC, so the user should check. Zimo, Lenz, ESU v4 and Hornby Sapphire support ABC, as do several other manufacturers. Most decoders require CV27 to be configured to a value of 1 to permit the ABC feature, but Lenz uses CV51 value 2, so always check the decoder's leaflet or manufacturer's specification list for that decoder.

How does it work? Put simply, one rail – always the right-hand rail depending on direction of travel – is isolated at both ends of the stopping section by inserting two plastic Insulated Rail Joiners (IRJs) or cutting gaps in the rail. The isolated section must be long enough to be able to bring the loco to a halt at the pre-set deceleration rate, and is fed from a network of five diodes, these being ideally Ultra-Fast versions such as UF4001 or UF4002. As the DCC loco moves into the section, the DCC wave form is reduced on the positive side via four of the diodes, each diode reducing the volts by 0.7 volts so that the four will reduce the rail volts by 2.8 volts; the other half of the cycle, the negative side, is reduced by 0.7 volts via the single fifth diode. This now asymmetric DCC signal causes the pre-set deceleration to take place and the loco slows to a stop. All lights and sounds, if fitted, remain operational.

When the distorted DCC wave form is replaced with the correct full value DCC wave form, the loco, under the control of its decoder's pre-set acceleration rate, moves off and gains speed. The diodes are removed from circuit by the operation of a conventional on/off switch or even a relay contact linking them out and restoring normal DCC. If a train approaches from the opposite direction, it simply continues as normal as the detection of the asymmetric DCC is dependent on the direction of travel.

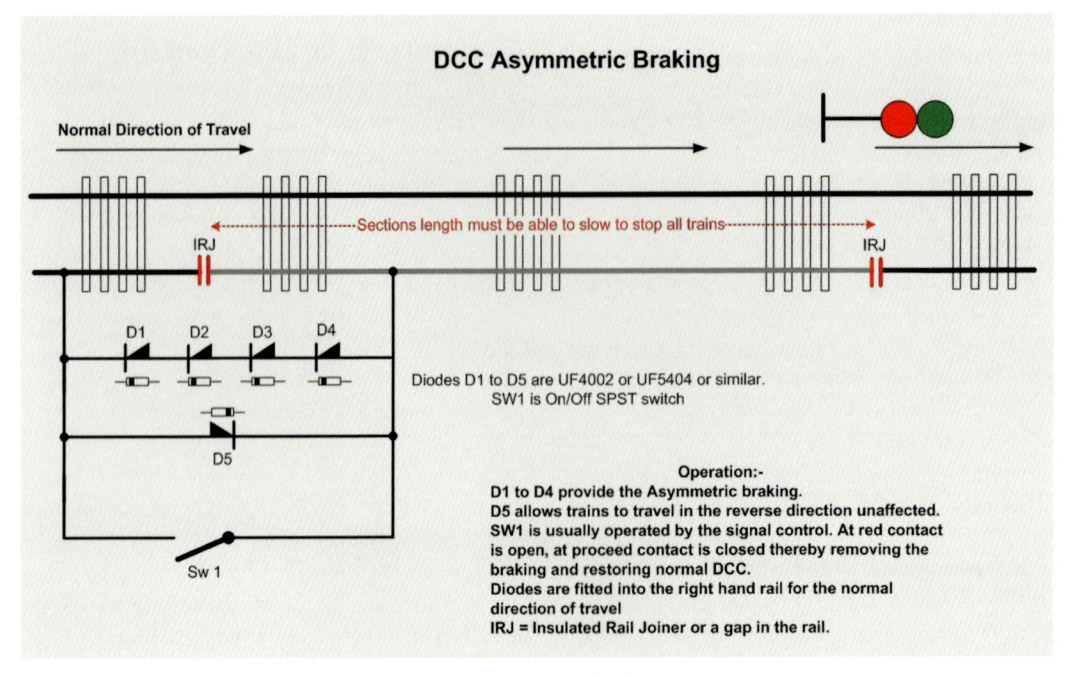

DCC Asymmetric Braking

Normal Direction of Travel

Sections length must be able to slow to stop all trains

IRJ   IRJ

D1 D2 D3 D4

Diodes D1 to D5 are UF4002 or UF5404 or similar.
SW1 is On/Off SPST switch

D5

Sw 1

Operation:-
D1 to D4 provide the Asymmetric braking.
D5 allows trains to travel in the reverse direction unaffected.
SW1 is usually operated by the signal control. At red contact is open, at proceed contact is closed thereby removing the braking and restoring normal DCC.
Diodes are fitted into the right hand rail for the normal direction of travel
IRJ = Insulated Rail Joiner or a gap in the rail.

DCC Asymmetric Braking

Wiring

How do you wire the command station or Booster to the rails? There are several methods, from simple plug-in power clips or powered track sections. But these must be designed for use with DCC, as some that are produced for DC operation have an internal capacitor fitted across their two input connections. These can be used with DCC, but must be converted or they will cause running problems. It is a simple matter to use a small flat-blade screwdriver and carefully flip open the plastic cover on either the plug-in power clip or the cover on the power track section and snip off the two wires from the capacitor and discard the capacitor, then close the cover; the clip is now able to operate with DCC. This is especially true for Hornby R602 and R8206 power connectors designed for DC.

However, best of all is to use dropper wires soldered to the rails. These wires can be soldered to the undersides of the rails before track-laying commences, or to the outer web area of the rails if the track has already been laid. The wire size used for droppers is normally a flexible single-core type – 16/0.2mm equipment wire is recommend. Smaller 7/0.2mm wire can also be used but with the proviso that the smaller wire's overall length from rail to bus wire is no more than 300mm.

A DCC bus pair is normally employed to feed all the rails, and runs around under the layout with the smaller 'dropper wires' tapped off and connected to the rails above. The input to the bus from the command station can be of a flexible type of wire, while the bus wire itself is solid. The minimum bus wire size I recommend is flexible 32/0.2mm equipment wire or 1.5mm^2 solid core. Of course, larger wire sizes can be used and will never cause harm. In fact, it is often better to use a larger wire size if available, and an increase in size will be needed for larger layouts where the length of the bus wire is greater, or where the command station or Booster offers a higher-output current. The main objective of the DCC bus pair is to provide the rails above with as many connection places as required, and to allow fault currents to rapidly return to the command station or Booster and cause the system to shut off the rail power. A coin dabbed momentarily on and off across the two powered running rails should immediately cause the

DCC system to trip and cut off the rail power. If this doesn't happen when the coin is touched across the rails, the cause should be investigated immediately and the system not used until the problem is corrected and the coin is proved to cause the system to trip.

How the connection is made between bus and dropper is entirely at the discretion of the layout builder. The best method is to twist or wrap the dropper around the bared bus wire, then solder the two wires together. Terminal block connectors, snap-lock splice connectors or tag strips are also often used. Common-connected two-, three- or five-way push-in-to-insert connectors are also making a headway, but these tend to be on the more expensive side. One such push-in is the Wago 221 connector, which accepts wires from 0.14mm to 6.0mm, so the bus and dropper wires can be connected to them without fear of loose connections. The bus not only feeds the output is taken to the input terminals of an all-electronic DCC circuit-breaker whose trip current has been adjusted to below that of the main console or Booster. The output of the circuit-breaker feeds a bus pair onto which all track rail droppers are connected. A second pair of bus wires also connects directly to the command station's 'Track' terminals and these two wires are connected to all the accessory decoders or DCC point motors only. Should a problem occur on the rails, e.g. a train is accidently driven into an unset point and causes a short circuit, the circuit-breaker cuts off the rail power, but the command station is still working, and the accessory decoder can still be accessed from the DCC system and the point moved over to remove the short. The train can then be driven onto the point or backed away as required. Without the dual bus system and circuit-breaker the entire system would have shut down until the offending loco was

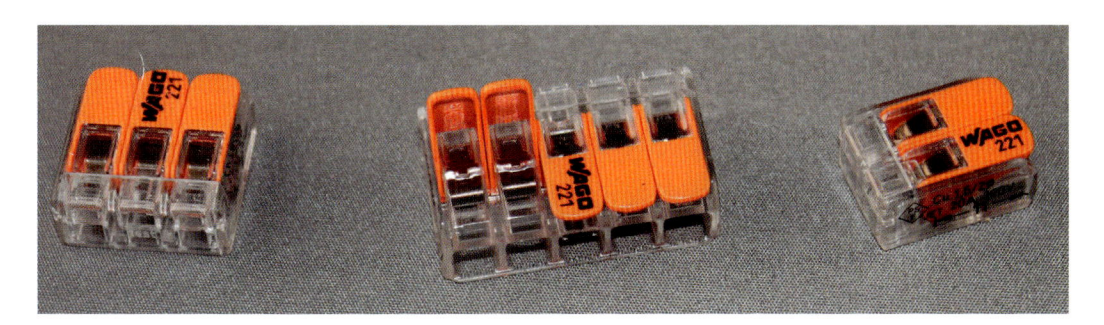

Three-way, five-way and two-way connectors. The orange levers are lifted up and the bared wire end inserted into the connector; when the lever is pushed closed the wire is gripped securely and firmly.

rails but all DCC accessory decoders too. Wago or similar connectors are common-connected internally, so one input wire feeds all the exit connections of that one connector.

The twin-bus system

Where point motors are fed from the DCC system via accessory decoders or DCC-fitted motors, the DCC layout can have two separate DCC bus wire pairs (a dual bus), which offers better control protection for the locos and rail feeds. Basically, a feed from the command station's 'Track' terminals or a Booster's manually pushed clear or the point operated over by hand to remove the short.

One such DCC all-electronic circuit-breaker is the PSX1, which can have its trip current adjusted to allow it to trip at a lower current than that at which a main command station is set. It has various tripping current levels from 1.27 amps to a whopping 19.1 amps. The trip current settings available will cover most DCC systems, except the very basic systems that offer an output of less than 1.3 amps. It is important that the two bus wires are not allowed to interconnect with

DCC Dual Bus

The basic idea of how the DCC dual bus operates.

each other via any accessory decoder or other possible connection. DCC point motors with automatic built-in frog switching such as the Cobalt iP Digital should not use terminal 3 for the frog switching. In this case the change-over contacts of the digital iP would be used with the track bus feeding into these contacts and the frog connected to the common change-over contact.

The approximate conversion sizes of some of the more commonly used wire sizes found in DCC wiring are as follows:

AWG	Area(mm²)	Metric standard
13	2.5	50/0.25mm
15	1.5	30/0.25mm
17	1.0	32/0.2mm
20	0.5	16/0.2mm
24	0.20	7.0.2mm

Some layouts will be improved by fitting DCC filters to the ends of the bus pair of wires that feed the rails. The filter consists of just two simple components: a ceramic 0.1uF capacitor and a resistor of a value of 120 to 150 ohms and rated at 2 or 3 watts. The two components cost less than £1 and are connected together in series with each other, one end of the resistor to one wire of the capacitor – it doesn't matter which way round they are connected as they are not polarity-conscious devices. The remaining end of the resistor and the capacitor wire are connected directly to the end of the track bus feed pair of wires, with one filter at all bus wire ends (see diagram opposite top).

Some DCC problems and fixes

- **Loco runs the opposite way to other locos, or to the DCC console's direction setting.** There are two methods available to correct this: 1) reverse the two motor feed wires on the actual motor terminals or 2) without opening the loco adjust CV29 increase by 1 if the existing value is an even number or reduce it by 1 if it is currently an odd number, e.g. read CV29=6 then make it 7, or read 7 then make it

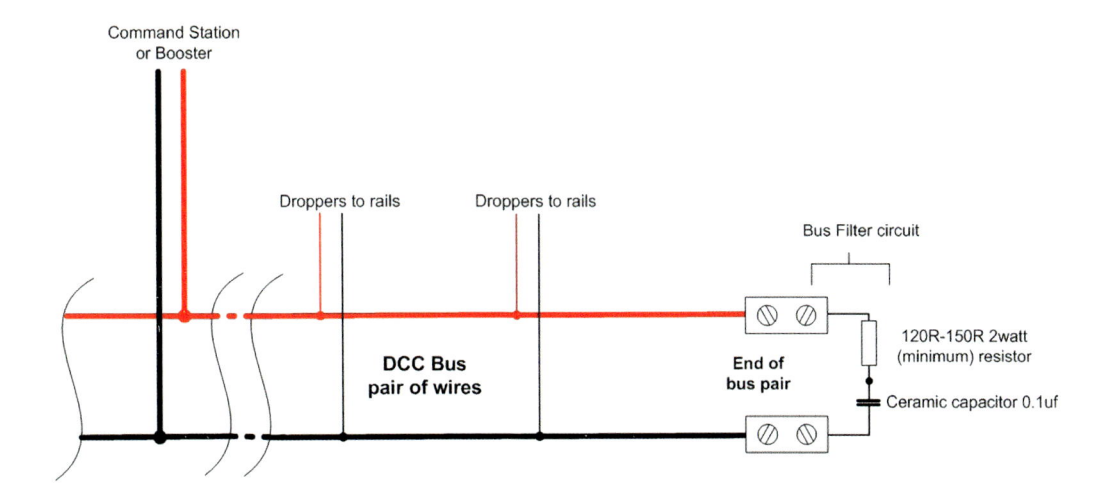

Use of DCC filters.

6. This permanently sets the direction of travel to the opposite way from what it was previously.

- **Loco suddenly takes off at full speed and is uncontrollable.** The decoder has 'seen' the full DCC rail volts as being DC and at full voltage. The decoder is 'confused' and applies full DCC rail voltage minus a little for conversion to DC to the motor. As decoders act on the last received instruction until they receive another, the decoder continues to apply full power to the motor. Often the only way to stop the errant loco is to remove rail power or physically take the loco off the rails. After ensuring all rail tops and wheel rims are spotlessly clean, this runaway problem can be corrected via CV29 and turning off the DC operation mode. This of course means that the loco can no longer be operated on a DC layout, but it does overcome the runaway problem. To turn off DC operation in a decoder, access the CV29 read current value and reduce it by 4 to that read, e.g. existing CV29 value is at 6 so reduce it to 2.

- **Loco is seen to skip or jump suddenly or gives generally poor running.** This is often due to the requirement to adjust CV54 and CV55. Try CV55 first as this is more likely to solve the problem. On some locos CV55 should be reduced if the loco has a big flywheel (or large worm drives with a lot of mass), or increased if it has no flywheel and/or smaller worm drives. The CV value would normally be in the range 0-63 or 0-255. Always check the decoder's manual for the CV value range settings. Adjust the CV setting by units of 5 or 10 at a time, then check the results.

  To further fine-tune the running of a loco's motor, CV54 can also be changed. Back EMF (Back Electro-Motive Force) basically reads the voltage produced by the motor when free running and puts pulses of power to the motor to try and keep it running at a continuous speed. If these are too strong, this too can lead to hunting or hesitancy. I would recommend initially trying to reduce this number. The CV value must be in the range 0-63 or whatever the decoder manufacturer has specified. Initially, I would suggest setting CV54 to about 10 and CV55 to around 60. If all else fails, remove all motor suppression capacitors (there may be more than one!).

- **Loco takes longer than expected to stop.** CV4 deceleration value is set high. Reduce CV4 to 1 and retest the loco. If deceleration is required, then increase the CV4 value to 5 and retry, then go up in units of 5 until the deceleration rate is correct or near to that wanted. Then adjust CV4 up or down from that setting in single units of 1 until the required level is reached.

- **Loco is slow to pull away.**

CV3 acceleration is set too high. Set CV3 to 1 and retest the loco. As for CV4, if acceleration is required increase CV3 by units of 5 and fine-tune after reaching the level needed by adjusting up or down by single units.

- **Loco is too slow or fast at maximum throttle.** Set CV5 top speed control to the decoder's maximum; this can be 63 or more normally 255, depending on the make of decoder. If it is too fast at full throttle setting, reduce CV5 value. Once CV5 is set, CV6 should be set to ideally 1/3 and no more than to 1/2 (one-third to half maximum) of the value set in CV5 to ensure a smooth throttle range. For example, CV5 is set to 200 therefore CV6 needs to be set to around 67 to 100 maximum. Note that some decoders do not offer CV5 or CV6 adjustments.

- **Loco is unresponsive or will not start although working properly previously.**

Initially check that it has not reverted to its default address number of 3. If still not responding, try resetting the decoder back to the 'as manufactured' default settings, including address number back to 3 and any other CVs. Many loco decoders are reset by CV8 entering a value of 8, but do check with the decoder manufacturer's leaflet or website, as some use differing CV numbers and values for a reset.

As with all CV adjustments, its very wise to read the decoder's leaflet to find out what CV number adjusts what operation – they may differ! Also read the CV value and make a note of it before undertaking any alterations; then if something is not correct you can return the CV value to where it was originally.

Using binary to configure Configuration Variables (CVs)

Author's note: This was originally written by an anonymous contributor, to whom thanks are due for allowing it to be reproduced here and amended by myself to reduce content.

The purpose of this section is to explain the relationship between binary and decimal numbering schemes and how this relationship is applied to the configuration of Configuration Variables (CVs) for DCC (Digital Command Control) model railway decoders, with particular focus on the DCC CV29 variable.

CV 'bits' and 'bytes'

Bit

The average computer uses two 'states' to compute data – the 'on' and 'off' states. In computer terms, the 'on' state is represented by '1' and the 'off' state by '0'. These '1s' and '0s' are termed 'bits' and use the binary method of calculations.

Byte

A 'byte' is the computing term given to a group of eight binary 'bits'. The term 'binary' is an adjective meaning 'relating to, composed of, or involving two things'.

In computing terms, a 'byte' contains 8 'bits' in a 'binary' two-state code.

The 8-bit byte in detail

In DCC, a CV (Configuration Variable) is represented as a decimal number between 0 and 255. In binary a decimal number between 0 and 255 can be represented by an 8-bit byte.

To help make this clearer, Table 1 is an 'aide memoir', or a 'look-up' table, that can be used to convert decimal to binary and binary to decimal. A byte is made up of 8 bits, and these bits are defined as Bit 7, Bit 6, Bit 5 and so on to Bit 0.

Each of these eight individual bits represents a decimal number as shown in the middle row of Table 1. Take the decimal number 88, for example; this is the summation of decimal numbers 64 + 16 + 8. If we place a '1' in the 'Binary' row of Table 1 for these three decimal numbers, and a '0' in the other 'Binary' row boxes, the Table 1 'Binary' row would read '0 1 0 1 1 0 0 0'; thus decimal 88 = binary 01011000.

If we have an 8-bit binary number (a byte) and we want to know what that number is in decimal, we populate the 'Binary' row of Table 1 with the '0' and '1' bits, then in the 'Binary' row boxes where a '1' is present we add the corresponding 'Decimal' numbers in the row above.

For example, using the previous 8-bit binary number (byte) of 01001101, the bottom 'Binary' row of Table 1 would be populated as ' 0 1 0 0 1 1 0 1'. Therefore, the numbers in the 'Decimal' row that have a binary '1' entered in the row below them are 64 + 8 + 4 + 1 = 77. Thus, binary 01001101 = decimal 77.

Using Table 1 it is therefore possible to convert any decimal number between 0 and 255 into a binary byte of 8 bits by adding together the decimal values of the Table 1 columns where the binary bit in the byte is set to '1'.

Table 2 extends this concept into a working example, showing the binary-byte-bit sequence for the decimal numbers 0 to 10 inclusive, plus 255. To fully understand the contents of Table 2, it would be helpful to look at the table in conjunction with Table 1.

Looking at the 'Binary' column of Table 2, it can be seen that there is a sequential and progressive pattern in the way that the binary '1s' and '0s' increment as the corresponding decimal number increases by 1. Therefore there are 256 possible combinations of 'binary byte' bit patterns – that is to say, decimal 0 plus decimal 1 to 255.

Table 1

Byte	Bit 7	Bit 6	Bit 5	Bit 4	Bit 3	Bit 2	Bit 1	Bit 0
Decimal	128	64	32	16	8	4	2	1
Binary	'0' or '1'	'0' or '1'	'0' or '1'	'0' or '1'	'0' or '1'	'0' or '1'	'0' or '1'	'0' or '1'

Table 2

Decimal	Decimal number derived from column decimal numbers added up where corresponding binary bit = 1	Binary
0	0 + 0 + 0 + 0 + 0 + 0 + 0 + 0	00000000
1	0 + 0 + 0 + 0 + 0 + 0 + 0 + 1	00000001
2	0 + 0 + 0 + 0 + 0 + 0 + 2 + 0	00000010
3	0 + 0 + 0 + 0 + 0 + 0 + 2 + 1	00000011
4	0 + 0 + 0 + 0 + 0 + 4 + 0 + 0	00000100
5	0 + 0 + 0 + 0 + 0 + 4 + 0 + 1	00000101
6	0 + 0 + 0 + 0 + 0 + 4 + 2 + 0	00000110
7	0 + 0 + 0 + 0 + 0 + 4 + 2 + 1	00000111
8	0 + 0 + 0 + 0 + 8 + 0 + 0 + 0	00001000
9	0 + 0 + 0 + 0 + 8 + 0 + 0 + 1	00001001
10	0 + 0 + 0 + 0 + 8 + 0 + 2 + 0	00001010
and so on to		
255	128 + 64 + 32 + 16 + 8 + 4 + 2 + 1	11111111

Working backwards: deriving an 8-bit binary byte sequence from a decimal number

As well as using Table 1 to derive the binary byte bits from the decimal number, we can achieve the same result in two further ways.

As a worked example, consider the decimal number 57. This time we start working from the left-hand side of the 8-bit byte (Bit 7):

Can we divide	57	by	128	
answer is	NO		thus Bit 7 = 0	
Can we divide	57	by	64	
answer is	NO		thus Bit 6 = 0	
Can we divide	57	by	32	
answer is	YES		thus Bit 5 = 1	
			(25 remaining)	
Can we divide	25	by	16	
answer is	YES		thus Bit 4 = 1	
			(9 remaining)	
Can we divide	9	by	8	
answer is	YES		thus Bit 3 = 1	
			(1 remaining)	
Can we divide	1	by	4	
answer is	NO		thus Bit 2 = 0	
Can we divide	1	by	2	
answer is	NO		thus Bit 1 = 0	
Can we divide	1	by	1	
answer is	YES		thus Bit 0 = 1	
			(0 remaining*)	

* If you don't end up with zero remaining in the very last bottom-row calculation, you have gone wrong somewhere with a previous division.

Therefore, reading from the top, decimal 57 = binary 00111001.

The same basic sequential process can be used to work back any decimal number between 0 and 255 into an 8-bit binary byte.

As an alternative to the method above, there is the 'divide by 2 method', which can do the same task.

In this method, the decimal number is divided by 2, so where the decimal number is 'even' the remainder left after division will be '0', and where the decimal number is 'odd' the remainder left after division will be '1'. These '0' and '1' remainders define the binary bits.

Here is an example using the same decimal number 57:

57 divided by 2 = 28 with 1 remaining
28 divided by 2 = 14 with 0 remaining
14 divided by 2 = 7 with 0 remaining
7 divided by 2 = 3 with 1 remaining
3 divided by 2 = 1 with 1 remaining
1 divided by 2 = 0 with 1 remaining

Once the division integer is zero (0), the division calculations stop. (An integer is a positive (or negative) whole number or zero.)

Now, taking the '0s' and '1s' from the 'remaining' column and writing the numbers *from the bottom up*, we get '1 1 1 0 0 1'.

But this binary string is not a full 8-bit byte because it has only 6 bits in it. To make it into an 8-bit byte we need to add additional 'padding' to make a total of 8 bits, in the form of leading '0s'. So the final binary number is '0 0 1 1 1 0 0 1'.

As can be seen, this is exactly the same result as that obtained in the first method – decimal 57 = binary 00111001.

Apply the above to DCC CV29

CV29 has up to eight features that can be either enabled or disabled by setting the appropriate 'bit' in the 'byte'. These 'bits' are like 'on/off' switches to enable or disable a feature.

The eight bits are shown in Table 3. To enable a specific feature in the table above, the corresponding bit in the 8-bit byte is set to 1. To disable the specific feature, the corresponding bit in the 8-bit byte is set to '0'. Some examples of common decimal values of CV29 are Decimal 2, 6 and 38; in binary these would be as shown in Table 4.

When looking at Table 4, relate the entries contained within it back to the contents of Table 3. So, for example, from Table 4 to only enable 28/128 Speed Steps + DC Operation you would write decimal value 6 to CV29.

Changing the decimal number of the CV changes the corresponding binary bit sequence, and this change defines what features are enabled and disabled.

Table 3

Byte	Bit 7	Bit 6	Bit 5	Bit 4	Bit 3	Bit 2	Bit 1	Bit 0
Decimal	128	64	32	16	8	4	2	1
Binary	'0' or '1'	'0' or '1'	'0' or '1'	'0' or '1'	'0' or '1'	'0' or '1'	'0' or '1'	'0' or '1'
Feature	Reserved for Custom manufacturer use	Reserved for Custom manufacturer use	Long Loco Address	Complex Speed Curve	Railcom	DC Operation	28/128 Speed Steps	Reverse Direction

Table 4

Binary	Decimal	Enabled features
00000010	2	28/128 Speed Steps
00000110	4+2=6	DC Operation + 28/128 Speed Steps
00100110	32+4+2=38	Long Loco Addresses + DC Operation + 28/128 Speed Steps

For example, if a loco travels in the wrong direction because the motor has been wired up to the DCC decoder 'back to front', you could take the loco apart, unsolder the wires on the motor, reverse them and resolder them. Or you could fix the issue in the DCC software by incrementing the value of CV29 by decimal 1. Refer to Table 3 ('Bit 0' column): by incrementing the decimal value of CV29 by decimal 1, the Bit 0 of the 8-bit byte is set to binary 1, which enables the 'Reverse Direction' CV29 feature.

Using the three examples in Table 4:

The CV29 decimal 2 value would become decimal 3
The CV29 decimal 6 value would become decimal 7
The CV29 decimal 38 value would become decimal 39

9
Special scenic effects

From anti-flicker carriage lighting to static grass, special effects help make the model come alive!

Carriage lighting

Carriage lighting or brake van rear lighting with anti-flicker can be produced for DC or DCC operation with the aid of a few readily available electronic components. The idea is that as the carriage or guard's van on a passenger or goods train passes over a section of track that may not be as clean as it should be or over the plastic frog area of insulated-frog points, the lighting remains on should the power be momentarily lost.

An electrolytic capacitor is charged and acts as a 'reservoir of power', releasing the stored power when no input is available from the rails/wheels. However, the problem is that on DC the rail polarity reverses with direction of travel, and on DCC it's a sort of AC, so the capacitor could be fed with the wrong polarity if directly connected across the rails/wheels, and this could cause the electrolytic capacitor to possibly explode! The answer is to add a bridge rectifier between the capacitor and the wheel pick-ups; this ensures that its output is always the correct way around to feed the capacitor, regardless of the DC direction of travel or the DCC supply.

Another problem can be encountered where several lighting units are used in more than one carriage, causing an in-rush of current drawn by all the capacitors trying to charge up at once at power switch-on. This in-rush current could cause the control system to see a large current flow and consider it as a short circuit or overload, and in turn this can cause the system's over-current device to operate. By adding a series resistor in one wire going to the bridge rectifier AC input, the in-rush current can be better controlled, and a 330-ohm (330R) resistor will aid this. The capacitor can now charge and act as the reservoir and feed the lighting.

Ideally the lighting itself is of the LED style, either a small red LED acting as a rear tail lamp on a brake van or as a group of white LEDs acting as the interior illumination of a passenger carriage. The interior illumination can be by several single white LEDs or by using an LED strip, often three LEDs, and a series resistor on a self-adhesive strip. These strips can also be supplied in multiple groups of three. Use warm white LEDs to represent filament lighting and white LEDs for fluorescent lighting in modern coaching stock. Do remember that LEDs are polarity-conscious devices and must be connected to the supply the correct way around. On single LEDs the longer lead is the anode or positive lead, and on strips the positive is normally marked by a plus (+) symbol. If dimming of the lighting level is required, add a 3,300 to 5,000-ohm (3K3 to 5K0) resistor in series with the LEDs in the positive feed wire. The final value of resistor in ohms will need to be found by trial and error, testing with various values of resistor used in series until the desired level of illumination is reached.

The connection between the metal wheel and the wiring can be by fine phosphor bronze strips lightly rubbing on the wheel's rear face, or by specially produced wheel lighting connectors. From this wheel connection, fine flexible wires take the rail power (DC or DCC) to the bridge rectifier's AC pair of terminals. Wiring from the capacitor is to the bridge rectifier's DC terminals. If possible, use a 25-volt-rated capacitor of around 1000uF minimum, but if you are absolutely sure that your rail voltage will never exceed 16, use a smaller (in physical size) 16-volt-rated capacitor.

Commercially made lighting units can be purchased for those who do not wish to make their own units. But making your own is a very cost-effective method per unit for the basic electronic components needed, excluding the wheel connection wipers.

this can be thick card or painted plastic, etc, ensuring that no light bleed occurs through the material or where any joints are made with other surfaces.

Filament lamps were used inside buildings for many years and can still be used, but their main disadvantages are the heat they generate and the power needed to feed them, especially where many lamps are lit at one time. Many filament lamps – 'grain of rice' (GoR) or 'grain of wheat' (GoW) are rated at around 60 to 70 milliamps each. When all the lamps are added together to provide several lit areas, this soon mounts up! Therefore LEDs have taken over the major role in illumination. Much like the carriage lighting mentioned previously, either single LEDs or the strip types can be used and, when used with suitable series resistors, they can be adjusted in brightness. Many LEDs will consume just a few milliamps, typically 10 milliamps per lit LED or less. Therefore many more can be connected to the power supply without overloading it. I always recommend

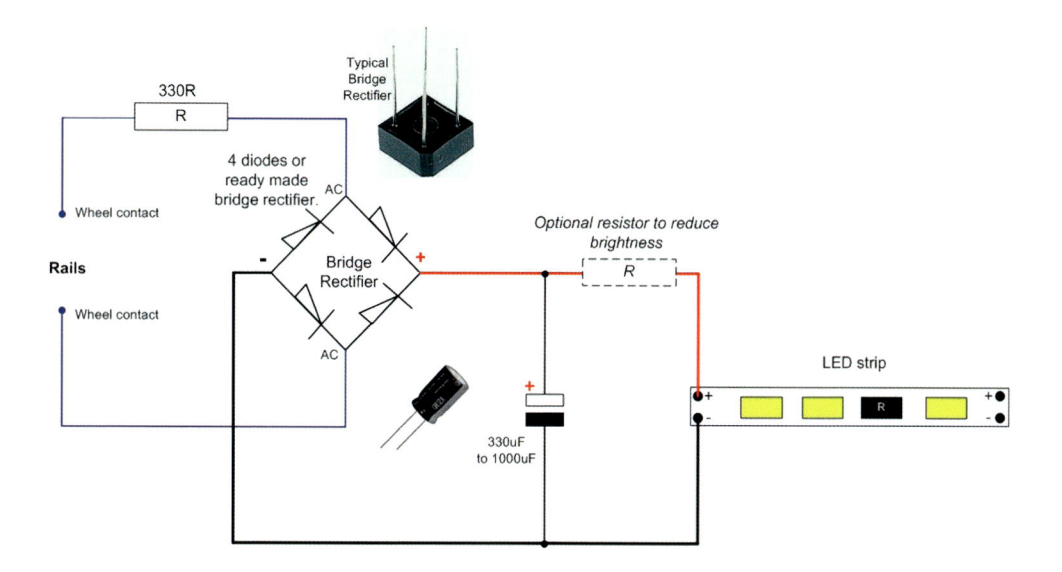

A typical arrangement for carriage illumination using an LED strip. The strip can be longer than shown and is normally made up into units of three LEDs. The circuit is suitable for both DC and DCC operation. The builder may wish to replace the bridge rectifier with four diodes, and for the DCC user it would then be wise to use fast-operation diodes such as UF4002 or other fast-recovery diodes.

Building lighting

Building lighting can be added to most buildings, whether card, plastic or cast resin. The main things to remember are not to light every room and to ensure that no light can escape through the walls (light bleed). The latter can be prevented quite often by applying a coat of paint to the inside of the building, and the former by sectioning off the inside of the building with light-resistance material;

using a regulated power supply rather than the uncontrolled output of a 'train controller'. The reason is that a regulated supply voltage remains at the stated constant level regardless of loading, whereas the train controller or an unregulated supply can vary widely in its output voltage. For example, a 12-volt DC supply that is unregulated can be 18 volts or more with no loading or very little load, and reduce to below 12 volts when loaded towards its maximum rating!

Always make sure that a series resistor is installed with any LED, as this will limit current to the LED and ensure that it operates correctly. Normally strip LEDs (see the accompanying illustration) will have a series resistor built into each group of three, but there is no reason why an additional resistor cannot be added to further reduce the brightness of the strip.

Obtaining LED strips in 3- or 5-metre rolls from auction websites or direct from China retailers is about the cheapest way I have found to obtain a good quantity. The strip is pre-marked with cut lines to allow three LEDs plus a built-in resistor to be used, or multiples of three can be used. Once cut into the required number of ways, solder the feed wires to the tabs at one end. These are usually marked '+' and '-' and polarity must be observed. Unless you are fitting them outside, I would avoid the waterproof LED strips sold as being suitable for outdoor use, as they are covered with a clear coating that makes cutting them and soldering feed wires more difficult.

Sequential or random building lighting can add to the overall effect whereby lights are switched on or off automatically suggesting dusk and dawn periods, or they can randomly switch on or off, all controlled by an electronic master circuit board onto which they are wired. Such control items can be a simple timer unit offering variable on and off periods, Arduino or Raspberry Pi micro-controllers, or complex computer-controlled DMX lighting effect controllers. Discussion of how these operate is not a part of this book, but further details can be obtained via internet searches.

Other lighting effects

Simple lighting controls for a one-off effect are readily available, and such devices can represent an arc welder at work, the arcing from the third rail as a train's pick-up shoe enters or leaves a conductor rail, or a camp fire flicker effect. Vehicle emergency beacon lights and road traffic light controllers are available in UK and continental styles. In fact, if it lights there is probably a module produced that will represent it! Ready-built modules are the simplest to use; however, more ambitious modellers who wishes to dabble in electronics can build their own modules using programmable Peripheral Interface Controller

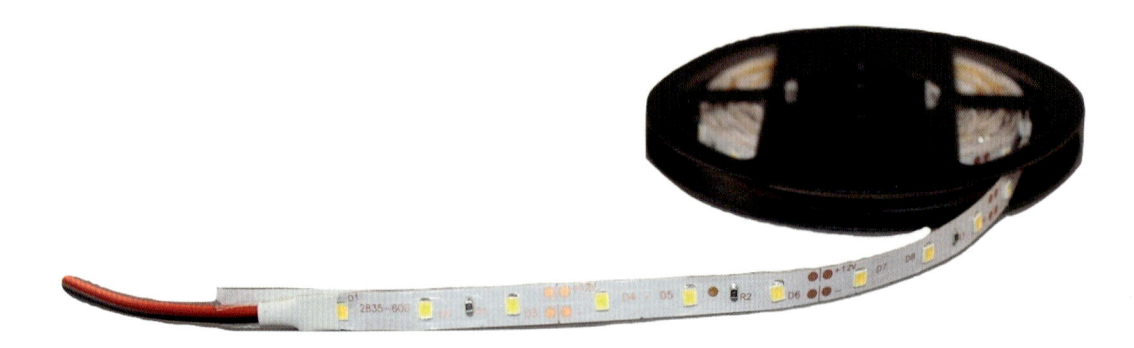

A typical roll of 5-metre-long warm white LEDs. In every group of three LEDS a resistor is factory fitted to the strip. A cut line is usually marked and is located between the four copper solder pad dots after every third LED. When uncut, each three LED section is automatically connected to the next section.

(PIC) micro-controller circuits. The output current available is low, coming directly from a PIC, but by allowing a transistor to be switched from that output the PIC's output can be increased via the transistor; an alternative is to use a relay, then its contacts to switch a load. Ready-made relay interface boards, ideally with an on-board Opto-coupler connection between the input and the relay coil, are cheaply available for direct operation from a PIC or micro-controller. Look for the 5-volt versions for general use with PIC or micro-controllers.

Electrically lit shop signs, both static, flashing or scrolling, are manufactured in various scales and are a simple 'plug and play' concept with the controlling electronics either built in or provided as a small circuit board to which the sign is connected.

Lighting station platform, goods yards, loco stabling areas and of course roads all adds to the character of the model when the room lights are dimmed and the layout illumination turned on. Street and station area lighting is sold in many forms, from modern street and platform lights to representations of gas lights. Many are LEDs and draw low power (current) from the supply. However, there are still a large number of ready-made filament lit lamps available, but the

An example of random lighting is illustrated in these three pictures, which show a 'Scout Hut Disco' in full swing! Note that the colour changes internally.

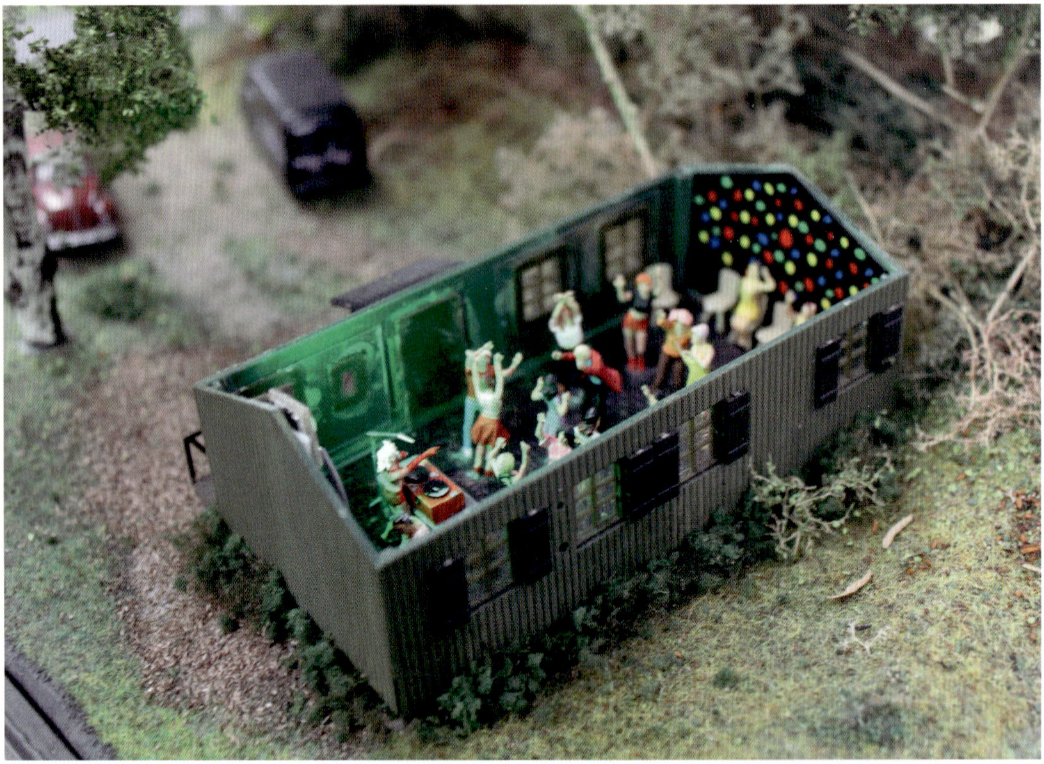

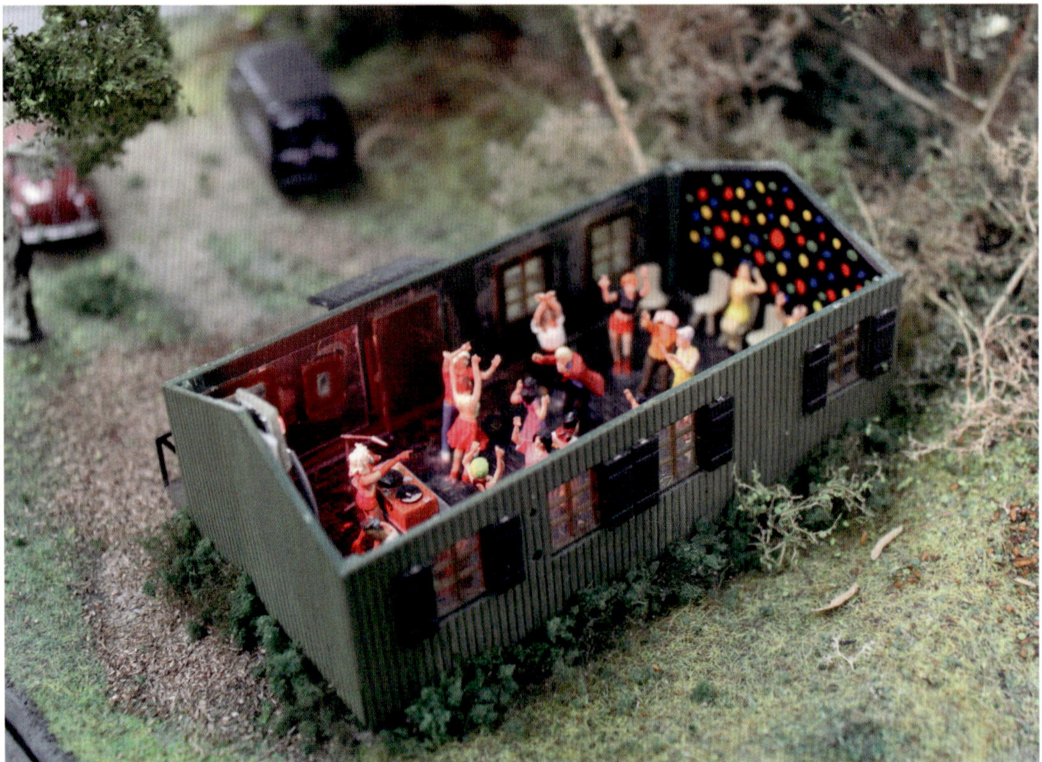

A typical four-way 5-volt interface board. Each relay has one set of change-over contacts. On this board the input is 5 volts DC and is made via the row of pins along the front right-hand edge. Opto isolators, one for each input/relay, separate the relay coil's operation voltage from the inputs for each relay. Normally the inputs are negative, but by moving a selector link they can be positive at the rated voltage, in this case 5 volts. Pins marked GND and VCC have a permanent 5 volts on them, GND being negative and VCC being positive. IN1 to IN4 pins are the inputs to operate each relay. The relays' contact connections are at the rear on the blue terminal blocks.

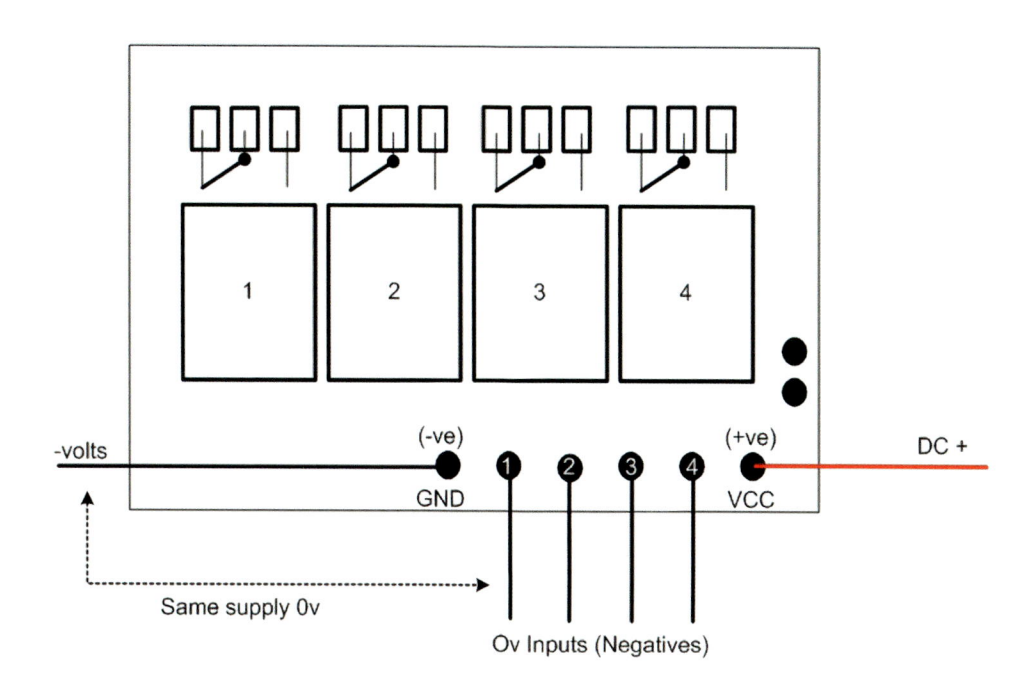

How the four-way interface board can be wired.

user should be aware of what is being obtained, as filament lamps will need far more power to allow multiples to operate. They also are prone to run hot – see above regarding GoW and GoR lamps. A separate power supply, which could also feed building lighting, is the ideal way of supplying power to these. I would always recommend opting for a DC regulated power source.

Electro-mechanically operated effects are also used – for example, a rabbit popping out of its burrow. Moving semaphore signal arms are common too. Both can be obtained ready-made or can be home-made to operate via a servo motor and control circuit board.

Static grass

Static grass is growing in popularity as the process helps to truly represent grass. In its simplest form it is applied to a base of wet PVA glue via a 'puffer bottle'; the bottle is loaded with fibres and, when pressed, produces the 'puff' and a static charge is generated as the puffer emits the grass fibres. However, a better effect is achieved by using a special static grass applicator tool. This normally looks either like a tea strainer, or a more expensive tubular device. Special static grass is sold in various lengths, and loaded into the 'tea strainer' or the hopper of the tubular device. PVA glue is spread over the area to be treated, and a pin or nail is inserted into the baseboard, ensuring that it passes through the wet PVA. The crocodile clip of the static grass device is connected to the pin or nail and when the button is operated to power the device a static charge is produced. As the fibres fall into the glue they stand mainly upright in it. By varying the length of the fibres long grasses can be represented with shorter grasses applied in other areas. When the PVA dries the grass fibres are held securely upright.

Home-made static grass application tools can be made from converted electric fly swats, or by using negative ion generators and a metal-mesh tea strainer or similar small mesh utensil; YouTube has several videos showing how to make these.

A good example of static grass applied to a cutting and hillside. The static grass fibres can be seen standing up. *Courtesy of Steve Mumford*

I would err on the side of caution for DCC users and recommend when using a static grass generator that any DCC-fitted locos are removed from the rails and kept off the layout – it may also be advisable to earth the rails. Certainly, do not have a DCC system powered up! But remember to remove the earth as soon as grassing work has ended! I haven't found any issues with static grass applicators, but I feel caution may be the better option than losing a loco's decoder or a static accessory decoder due to possible static charge leakage!

A commercially produced static grass applicator.

I made this static grass applicator a few years ago. It runs off a couple of AA batteries in the handle.

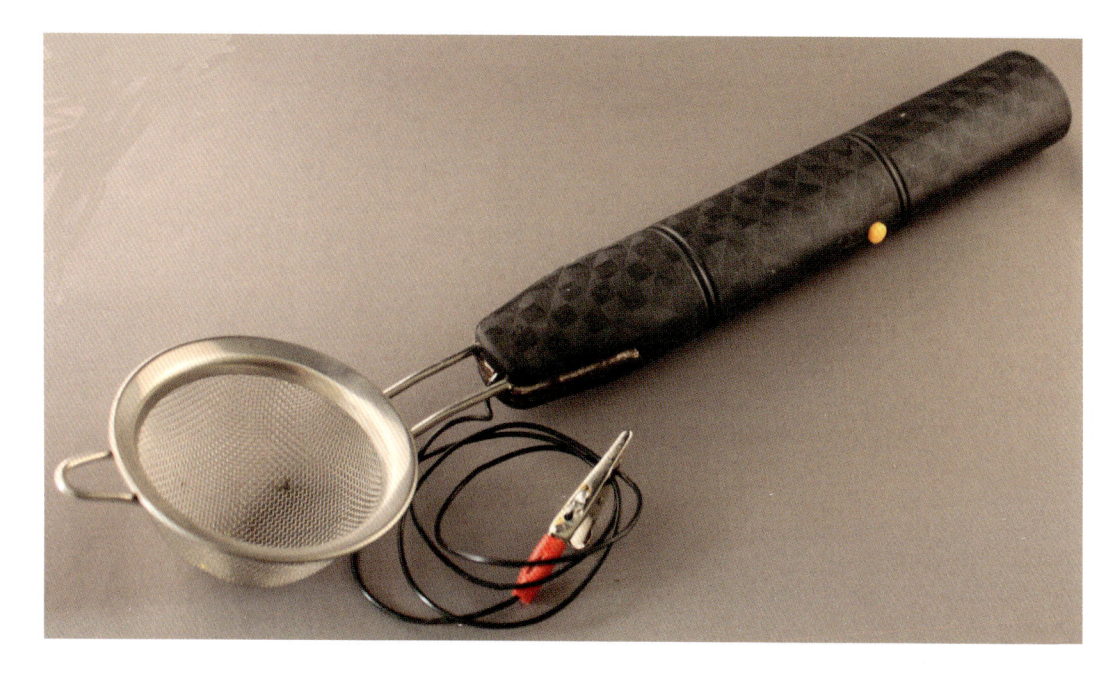

10
Basic electronics

I must at the outset advise the reader that I am by no means an electronics engineer, but I have an understanding of the basics and build items that help with train control and automation. For more detailed electronic circuits I would direct the reader to specialist books written in their entirety for railway modellers and hobbyists.

Some basics first.

Power source

Most electronics requires a stable and smooth DC power source. This can be from a battery, a regulated DC power supply or, at times, a USB connection. AC can be used, but will need to be converted to DC via a full wave rectifier, then a smoothing capacitor is added across the DC output. Many circuits will also add a voltage regulator to ensure that the output volts are 'clamped' to whatever the regulator is set to. Voltage regulators are explained later in this chapter.

Our power is normally referenced in wiring diagrams as VCC and zero (0) volts. VCC is the positive full voltage of the circuit, while zero volts, or 0 volts, is frequently the negative. Note that the negative can also be referenced as VSS. However, where a split or dual supply is used it can have a + VCC (positive) and a - VCC (minus negative) with a common zero volts, which is occasionally referred to as 'ground' – note that this is not the earth. The basic two styles are shown later under the regulated power supply heading.

Resistors

This is a device that has an ohm or resistance value and is added to a circuit to reduce current and voltage to a predetermined level as calculated. The ohm value of resistors is set in predefined value steps known a 'E' values, which were agreed in the 1950s and are still upheld today. The ohm value of an available resistor is therefore set by its E ranges of E3, E6, E12, E24 and E48, E96 and E192. The higher the E range number the more resistor values are available in that range. Additionally, the E number also denotes the tolerance values allowed for a resistor. E3 is 50% tolerance, while E6 is 20%, E12 is 10%, E24 is 5% and E48 is 1%. That is the amount by which the resistor's ohm value is permitted to be above or below the stated value. As an example, an E12 range resistor of 100 ohms has a 10% tolerance, so its actual value can be anywhere between 90 and 110 ohms. These tolerance ranges are normally 1%, 2%, 5%, 10% and 20%, and are denoted by a coloured band at the end of the resistor – 1% is brown, 2% red, 5% gold, 10% silver, and 20% has no markings. In most uses the modeller can ignore E3, which is now generally no longer available, and the E6 range, which are very limited in the values available and are now considered mainly out of date. All resistors in each E range are to a decade value. For example, E12 range resistors will be found in ohm values of 1.0, 1.2, 1.5, 1.8, 2.2, 2.7, 3.3, 3.9, 4.7, 5.6, 6.8 and 8.2 (12 set ranges). These then increase in decades, so for example 2.2 ohms is also in E12 range as 22, 220, 2200, 22000, 220000 and 2200000 ohms. Therefore the largest E12 value resistor in that E12 decade range is 2.2 million ohms, or 2M2. Circuits will then use either 'R', 'K' or 'M' to help prevent long digits having to the written, so for example 330 ohms will be shown as 330R, while 3,300 will have a 'K' for kilo (1,000) and be shown as 3K3; note that the 'K' moves to replace the decimal point, so it is

4-Band Code
560K Ω ±5%

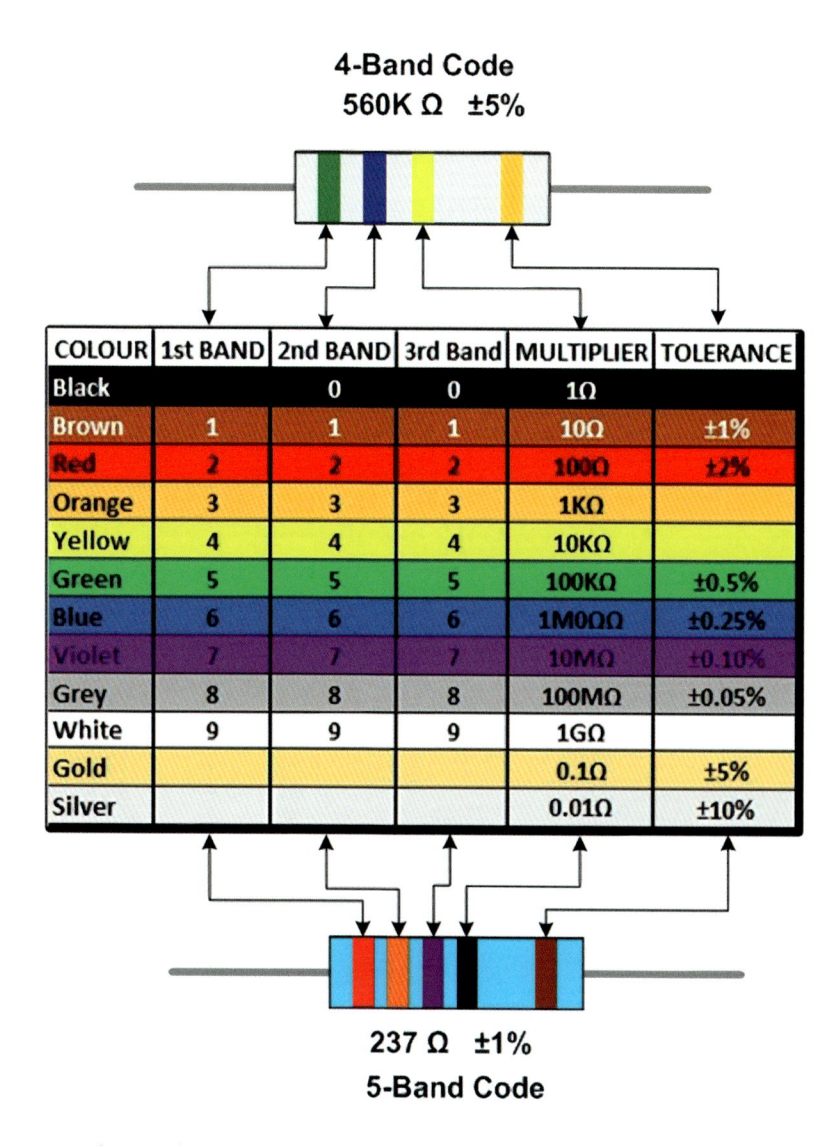

COLOUR	1st BAND	2nd BAND	3rd Band	MULTIPLIER	TOLERANCE
Black		0	0	1Ω	
Brown	1	1	1	10Ω	±1%
Red	2	2	2	100Ω	±2%
Orange	3	3	3	1KΩ	
Yellow	4	4	4	10KΩ	
Green	5	5	5	100KΩ	±0.5%
Blue	6	6	6	1MOΩΩ	±0.25%
Violet	7	7	7	10MΩ	±0.10%
Grey	8	8	8	100MΩ	±0.05%
White	9	9	9	1GΩ	
Gold				0.1Ω	±5%
Silver				0.01Ω	±10%

237 Ω ±1%
5-Band Code

Standard resistor colour coding.

shown as 3K3. A 33,000-ohm resistor would be shown as 33K and 330,000 is shown as 330K; finally 3.3 million ohms is shown as 3M3.

Resistors will normally be colour-coded and reference to the banding is essential to ensure the correct value of resistance is being used. Equally a resistor can be quickly checked by the use of a multimeter set to its continuity (ohms) range and the leads connected to the resistor. Note that this is best done with the resistor removed from the circuit, as it is very easy to get false readings from other components on a circuit board! Never try to check a resistor's value with a circuit powered up!

The accompanying table shows the common E12 resistor values.

Resistors come in two main styles, fixed value and variable value. The latter is usually known as a potentiometer, or 'pot' for short, and will have a set top value ohm range; by turning the shaft or moving a slider up or down the resistance is adjusted from minimum to maximum.

The adjustable wiper's position on the variable potentiometer sets the resistance value on the 'W' pin connection. By turning

Fixed value resistor symbol

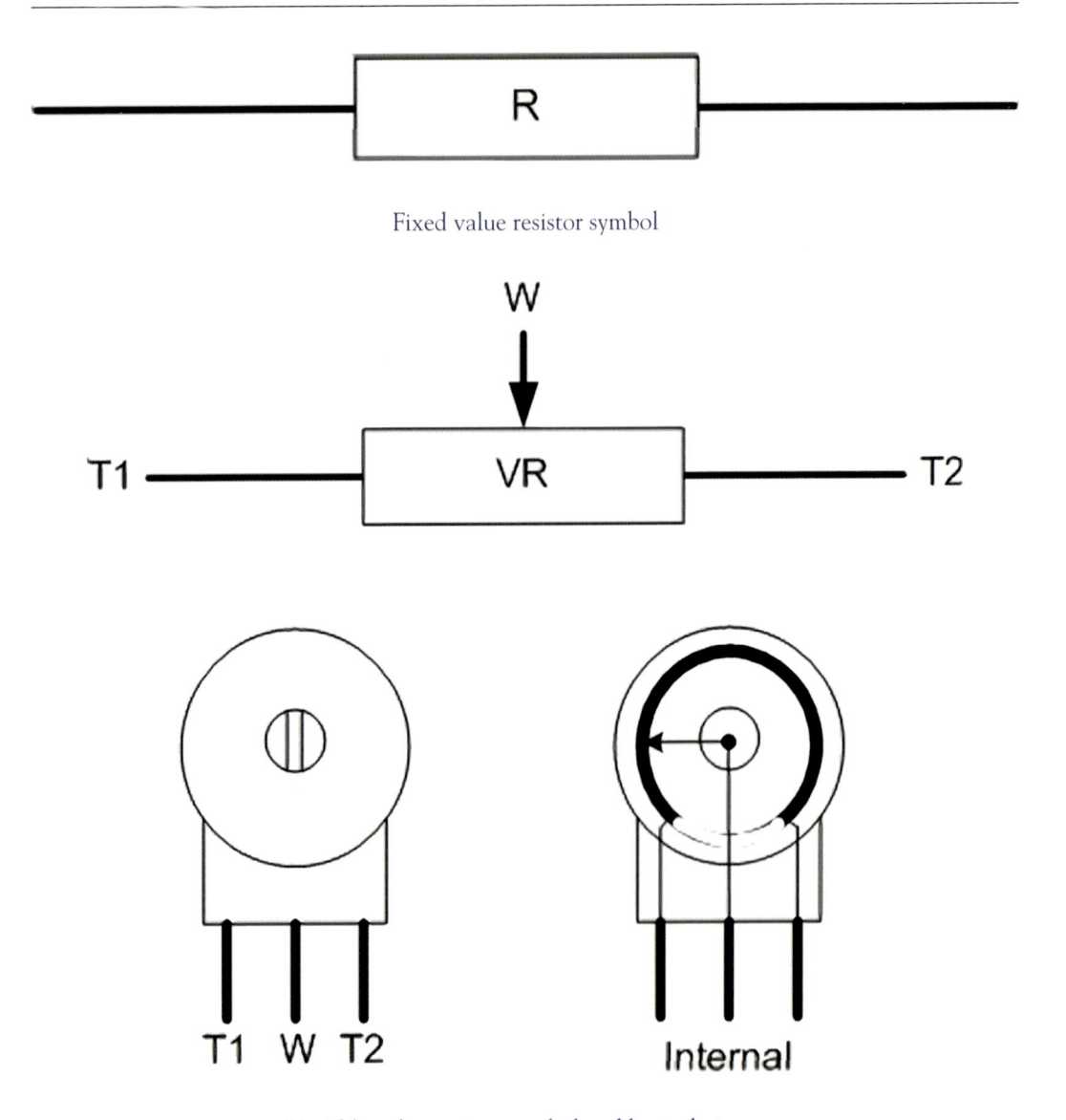

T1 W T2   Internal

Variable value resistor symbol and basic design.

the wiper, more or less resistance is inserted into the circuit. The resistance value of the variable resistor is that measured across T1 to T2. So for example a 5K variable resistor can be set to anywhere in the range of 0 (zero) to 5,000 ohms. Variable resistors come in two defined resistor adjustment types: linear and logarithmic. The linear resistor has a constant resistance all along the track, so the wiper's position is proportional in ohms to its position. These are usually referred to as Type A. The other style is 'log' or logarithmic, and is Type B, more suited to audio applications.

Capacitors

Again, much like resistors, capacitors are available in preset ranges, and are sold in values of a Farad. A Farad is a fairly large amount of capacitance and is rarely used except in so-called Super Capacitors, where values are often found in Farads. The values of capacitors are normally in micro-Farads (µF – 1 millionth of a Farad), nano-Farads (nF – 1,000 millionth of a Farad), and Pico Farads (pF – 1 million millionth of a Farad). Capacitor values can be marked in one of two ways. For example, 100nF is the same as 0.1µF.

The working voltage of a capacitor is usually of great importance, and if exceeded can result in failure of the capacitor. The working voltage of a capacitor defines the maximum continuous voltage that may be applied across it. This is normally printed on the case, or will be in the datasheet. The voltage normally refers to the largest DC voltage that can be applied to that capacitor. Be aware that when a capacitor is operating on a circuit with an AC waveform superimposed on a DC voltage, the voltages experienced may be well above the DC rated value, in which case the capacitor's rated DC voltage needs to be increased to at least 1.4 times that of the RMS measured AC voltage.

The two major types of capacitor that will be encountered are the electrolytic (polarised) and the ceramic or mica (non-polarised). Polarised capacitors have to be connected the correct way around on the circuit, but non-polarised can be fitted either way around. Generally, electrolytic capacitors are used to smooth AC ripple on a DC circuit or to store power for short periods. Typical examples in the model railway field would be as a power supply used to feed electronics where as much of the AC ripple part of the supply is needed to be removed after rectification, or in a Capacitor

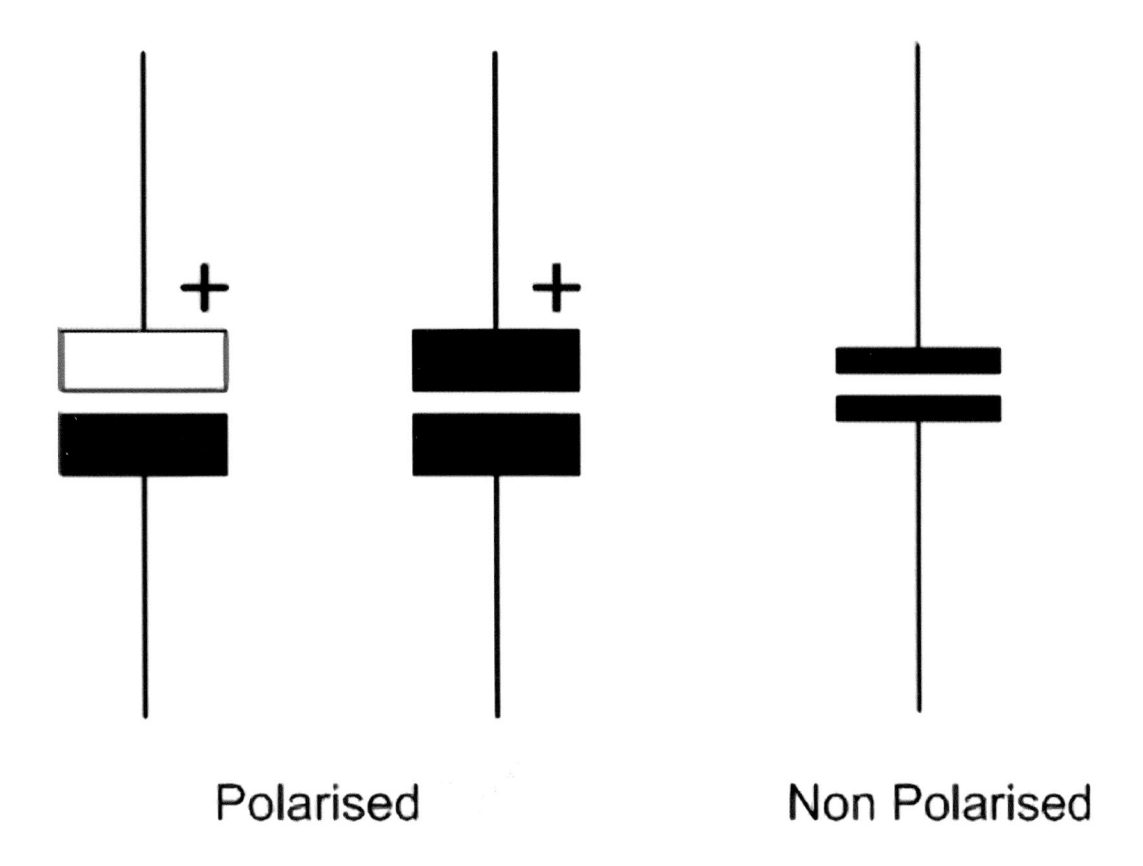

Polarised   **Non Polarised**

Typical schematic drawing symbols for electrolytic (polarised) and non-polarised capacitors. The left-hand symbol is mainly used in the UK and European circuit diagrams, while the middle version tends to be more frequently used in US wiring diagrams. The plus symbol can at times be omitted on the electrolytic European version. To add to the confusion, and very similar, is the version on the right, shown with thinner solid plates but without the plus symbol, which is used for non-electrolytic capacitors such as ceramic types or other non-polarised capacitors; occasionally the lower plate of the non-polarised symbol is shown as a crescent, or the ends are shown in a slight downward curve.

Discharge Unit (CDU) used to operate solenoid point motors, where power is stored and released as a pulse when required. Ceramic non-polarised capacitors are frequently used across a loco's electric motor to help remove Radio Frequency (RF) interference caused by the sparking of the motor brushes on the motor commutator. Alternatively they can be fitted inside a DC track power connector to help prevent any arcing interference that has occurred between rail and wheels, then being able to use the rails and associated wiring as a long antenna (aerial).

As stated, a standard electrolytic capacitor must be connected to the supply the correct way round. Failure to observe this will normally lead to the capacitor exploding! The negative lead is normally the shorter one and the side

A selection of electrolytic capacitors.

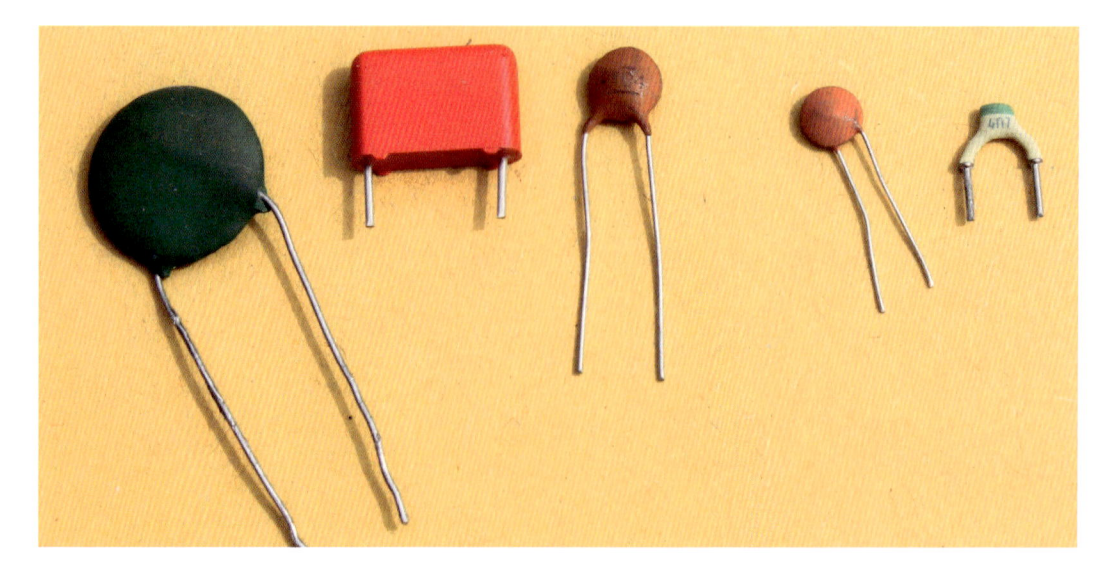

A selection of non-polarised capacitors.

of the electrolytic capacitor case is usually marked with a negative marking directly next to the negative lead. Never connect a standard electrolytic capacitor directly to an AC power supply.

Diodes

A diode in its most basic form can be considered like a one-way valve to the flow of electrons. Current flows through the diode in one direction only, from anode to cathode. If the flow is reversed the current is blocked. It is important not to exceed the diode's rated voltage or current as it will quickly become stressed and fail.

For use on model railways two types of diode will usually be encountered, conventional and light-emitting. Conventional diodes can be broken down into two main styles, standard silicon and high-speed. High-speed will be able to deal with high-frequency operations such as those encountered on a DCC (digital) layout, while the standard diode is frequently used to convert AC to DC, either by half wave or full wave rectification. Diodes are normally marked at their cathode end by a band of colour, frequently a silver or white band on an all-black body.

Light Emitting Diodes, or LEDs, are similar, but emit light – visible or infrared. However, they are not very good at blocking reverse current flow and have a much lower threshold for this than a standard diode. Their advantages are a low operating current, reasonably adjustable light output, cool running temperature and longevity when compared to filament lamps.

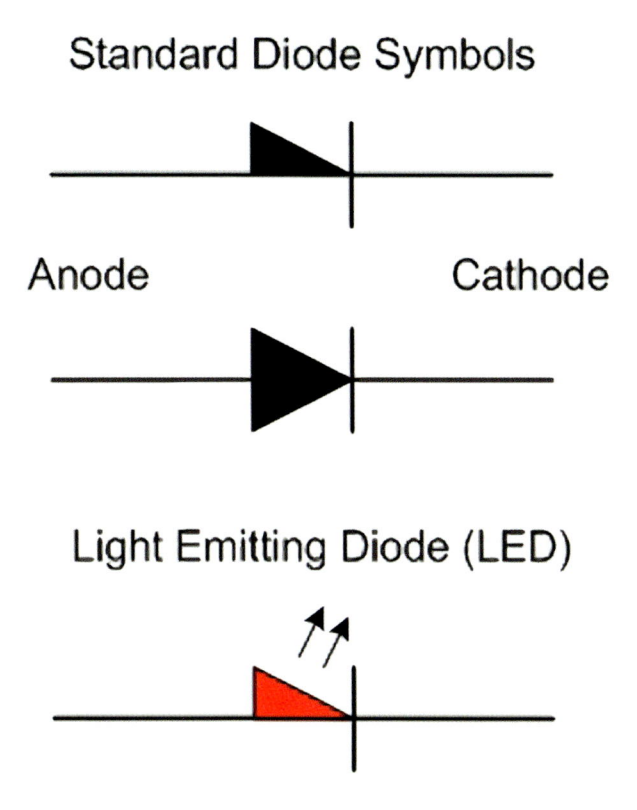

Standard and light-emitting diode symbols.

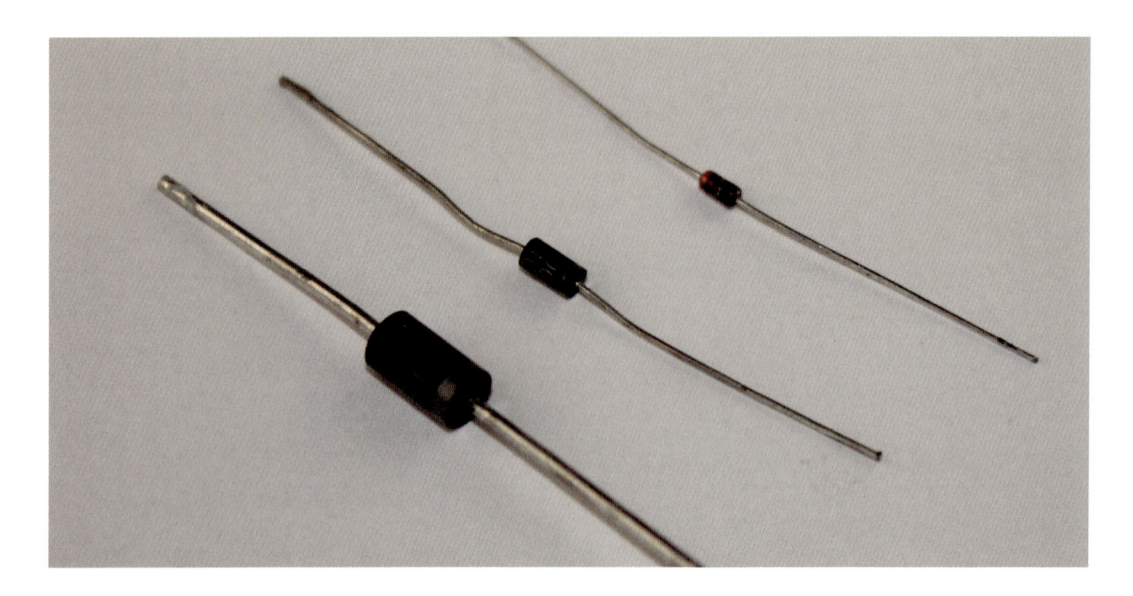

A selection of diodes. On the left is a 1N5401, in the middle a 1N4001 and furthest from the camera a 1N4148. They all do the same job but they handle different voltages and currents. The silver-banded end denotes the cathode (negative) end of the diode.

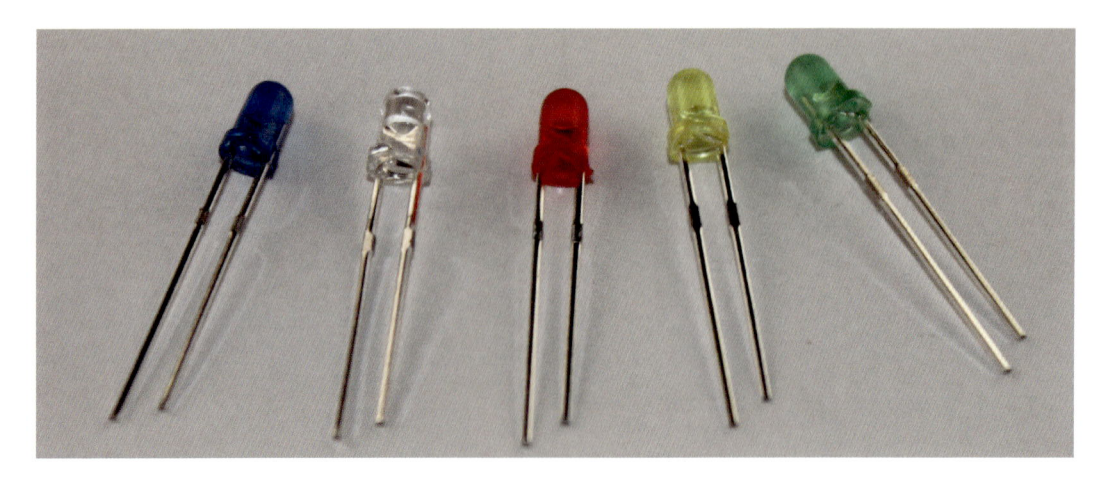

Assorted 3mm LEDs. Note that the longer lead is the anode (positive).

Transistors and integrated circuits

The transistor has been with us since around 1950 and gained a major hold in the electronics industry from around the mid-1960s. It can switch a current on or off or operate as an amplifier; it is also used to increase the gain in a circuit by adjusting the base voltage. There are far too many variations of transistor to begin making comparisons here, but they fall into two major types – NPN or PNP – that is Negative/Positive/Negative or the opposite, Positive/Negative/Positive. Both do similar work and the choice is determined by how the transistor is connected into its overall circuit. Generally the standard transistor will have three leads: collector, base, and emitter. Basically, the collector 'collects' the charge, the emitter 'emits' the charge, and the base is the control by which the transistor is switched on or off. With the NPN transistor, when a positive current flows through the base emitter junction,

Basic electronics

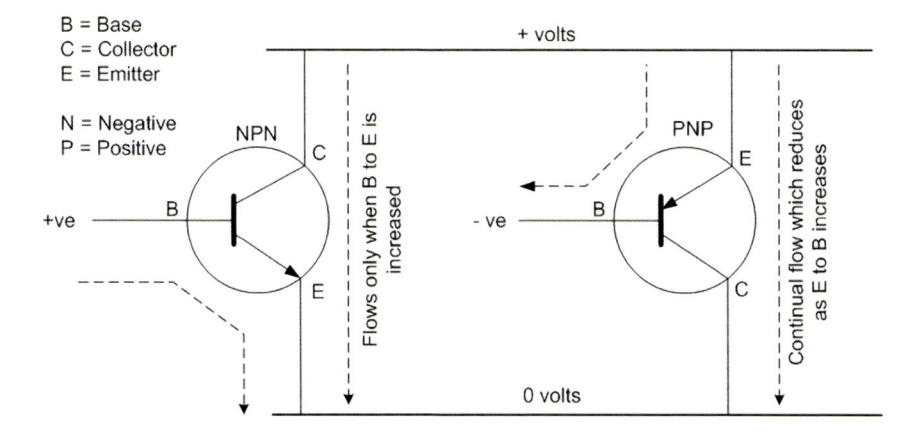

B = Base
C = Collector
E = Emitter

N = Negative
P = Positive

NPN: +ve → B; C at + volts; E at 0 volts. Flows only when B to E is increased.

PNP: B → -ve; E at + volts; C at 0 volts. Continual flow which reduces as E to B increases.

The standard diagrammatic symbols for both NPN and PNP transistors.

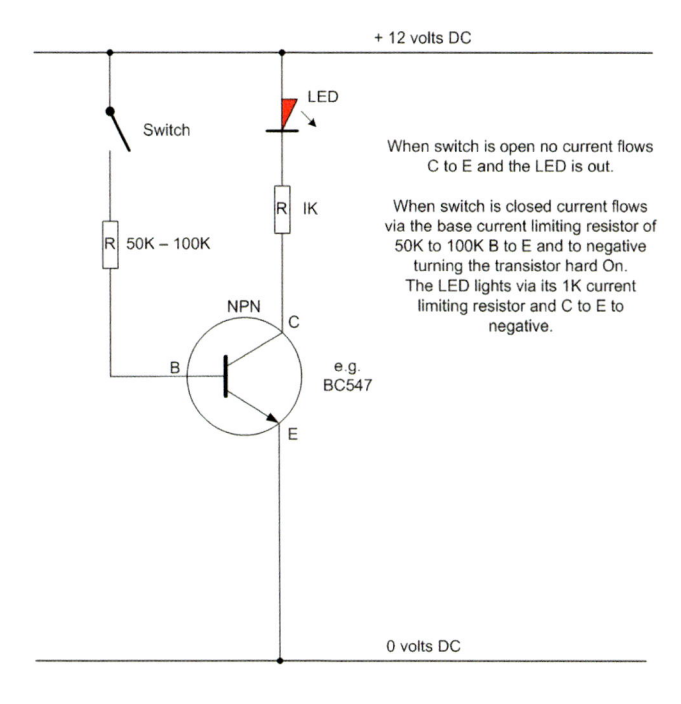

Circuit: +12 volts DC rail with Switch and LED (with R = 1K) feeding collector of NPN transistor (e.g. BC547). Base connected via R = 50K–100K through switch. Emitter to 0 volts DC.

When switch is open no current flows C to E and the LED is out.

When switch is closed current flows via the base current limiting resistor of 50K to 100K B to E and to negative turning the transistor hard On. The LED lights via its 1K current limiting resistor and C to E to negative.

Above and top right: Simple examples of a transistor doing the same job – switching a device on or off. Here they are being used to operate an LED and a relay.

electrons leave the emitter and flow into the base. As a result, most of the electrons are then able to flow right through from the emitter into the collector, attracted by the positive potential. The more the base is supplied with current, the harder the transistor turns on. This description is very basic and is not meant to form a tutorial on the workings of a transistor! Electrons flow in the opposite direction to current! However, unfortunately it not quite that simple, as you need to calculate the base resistor value to allow the point of saturation to fully turn on the transistor. The PNP transistor requires a negative base to allow it to turn off.

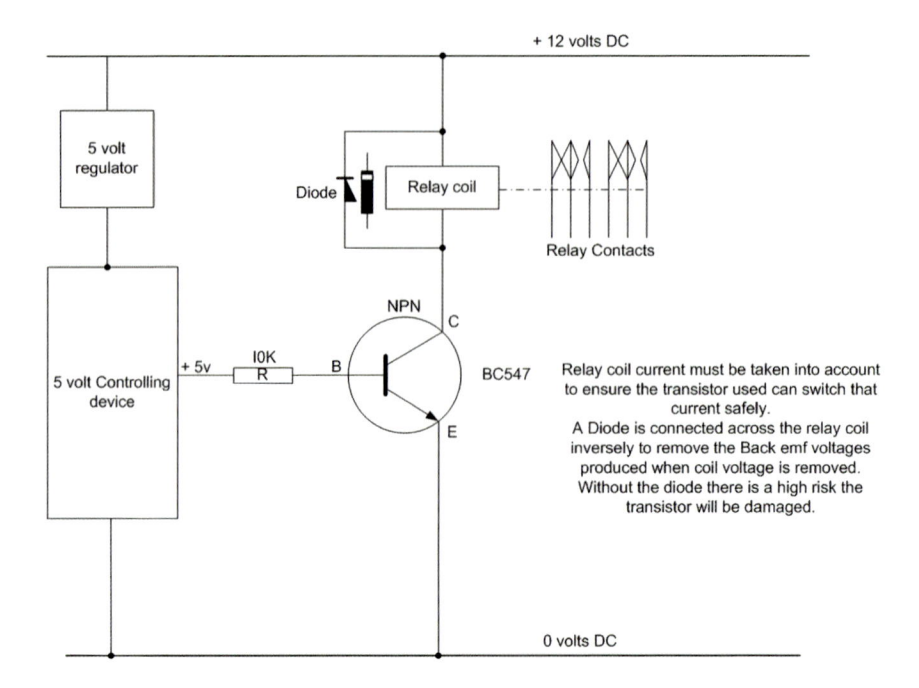

[Circuit diagram: Relay driver circuit with +12 volts DC supply, 5 volt regulator, 5 volt Controlling device, 10K resistor (R) at base of NPN BC547 transistor, relay coil with protective diode, and relay contacts.]

Relay coil current must be taken into account to ensure the transistor used can switch that current safely.
A Diode is connected across the relay coil inversely to remove the Back emf voltages produced when coil voltage is removed. Without the diode there is a high risk the transistor will be damaged.

Integrated Circuits (ICs) are simply many transistors placed inside a package. How they work and what they operate will depend on the type of IC. Some are used for switching, some for amplification, and others for inverting their input to the output. Some store messages such as data and keep it stored even when powered off, while others simply operate only when the power is turned on. Again, what and how ICs operate is too a vast field for this book to cover, so if the reader wishes to gain more knowledge a wealth of information is available on the Internet or in specialist electronics books.

A simple circuit that the modeller may find useful is a voltage regulator, which keeps the output voltage at a constant level. It uses a bridge rectifier, electrolytic capacitors, a ceramic capacitor and a fixed-voltage regulator. It should also use a heat sink of suitable metal – aluminium is frequently used for this purpose.

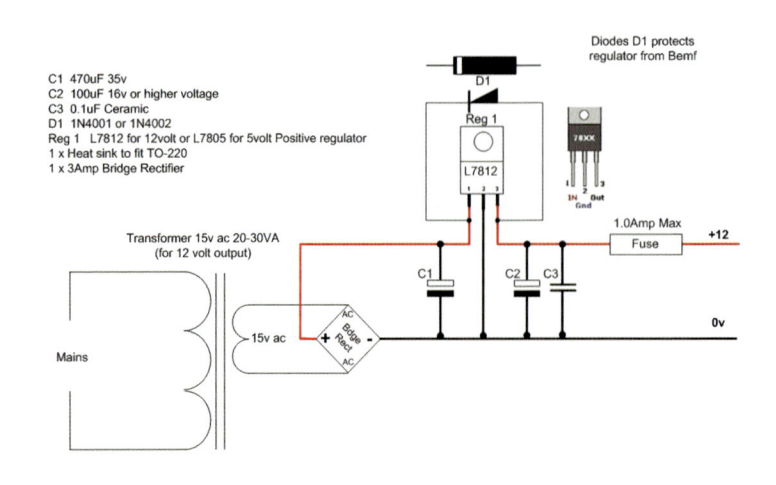

[Circuit diagram: 12-volt voltage regulator circuit with transformer, bridge rectifier, L7812 regulator, capacitors C1, C2, C3 and protective diode D1.]

C1 470uF 35v
C2 100uF 16v or higher voltage
C3 0.1uF Ceramic
D1 1N4001 or 1N4002
Reg 1   L7812 for 12volt or L7805 for 5volt Positive regulator
1 x Heat sink to fit TO-220
1 x 3Amp Bridge Rectifier

Transformer 15v ac 20-30VA (for 12 volt output)

Diodes D1 protects regulator from Bemf

This basic 12-volt voltage regulator circuit provides 12 volts DC at up to 1.0 amp when suitable heat sinking is fitted. It needs an input of around 14 to 16 volts AC or more and can also be DC at a higher voltage than the output required. When AC input is used, the rectifier converts it to DC and stabilises the output. Note that fixed-output regulators are available in several fixed-output voltages, and 9- or 5-volt regulators are also frequently used.

The bridge rectifier converts the AC to DC, and the first electrolytic capacitor smoothes the ripples after rectification. The DC positive is then fed to the input pin 1 of the regulator, and its output pin 3 feeds out to provide the stable 12 volts DC. Another electrolytic capacitor provides even further smoothing. Finally, a ceramic capacitor provides added stability by removing much of the high frequencies that may appear on the output to finally provide a near perfect DC supply. Negative (0v) DC flows directly through from the bridge rectifier. Pin 2 of the voltage regulator also connects to this negative.

By altering a few components, the fixed-voltage regulator circuit shown previously can be made to become voltage-adjustable on its output, depending on the setting of a variable potentiometer. Here a different regulator is used, and added to the circuit is a fixed-value resistor and a potentiometer to adjust the output volts.

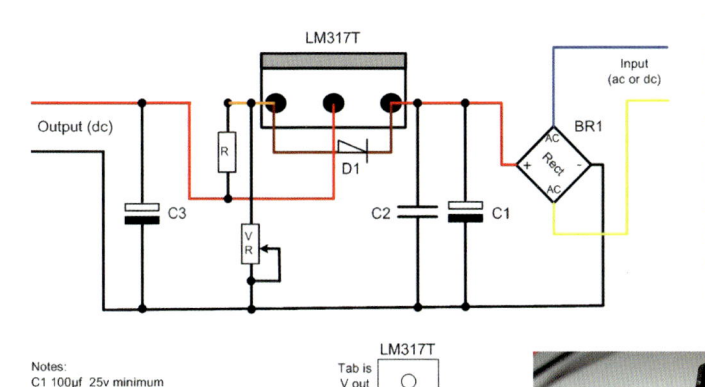

Notes:
C1 100µf 25v minimum
C2 0.1µf Ceramic
C3 100µf 25v minimum
D1 1N4001
R 220R 0.25w
VR 5K multi turn Cermet
Voltage Reg LM317T
BR1 Bridge rectifier
Heatsink for T220 case device

The circuit diagram is also shown in the photograph built onto a piece of stripboard. Voltage adjustment is via the small grub screw on the blue potentiometer. In both cases the input voltage must be around 2.0 volts greater than the required output voltage, e.g. for 12 volts output an input of a minimum of 14 volts is required.

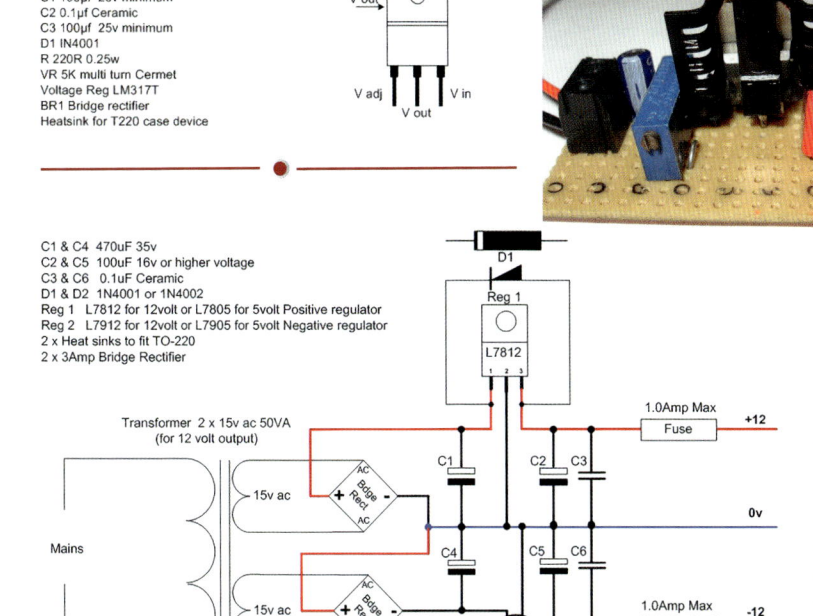

C1 & C4 470uF 35v
C2 & C5 100uF 16v or higher voltage
C3 & C6 0.1uF Ceramic
D1 & D2 1N4001 or 1N4002
Reg 1   L7812 for 12volt or L7805 for 5volt Positive regulator
Reg 2   L7912 for 12volt or L7905 for 5volt Negative regulator
2 x Heat sinks to fit TO-220
2 x 3Amp Bridge Rectifier

Transformer 2 x 15v ac 50VA (for 12 volt output)

Diodes D1 & D2 protect regulators from Bemf

NOTE differing pin arrangements

For those needing a dual output supply offering a positive, zero and negative voltage, a dual-wound power supply is required, and the use of a negative voltage regulator is recommended. The circuit is shown here and is similar to that of the fixed regulator but with added components.

A spot face cutter tool and a piece of stripboard.

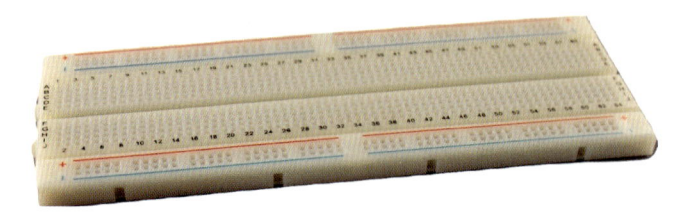

A small 'bread board'. This makes an excellent project board for constructing and testing a circuit before soldering it to a stripboard.

I would highly recommend that the electronic experimenter obtain a 'bread board', which is used to easily assemble components and carry out checks and tests before building the final circuit on stripboard or similar PCB material. When using stripboard, the copper tracks will need to be cut through at strategic locations to stop current flowing into that part of the circuit where it is not required.

The copper needs careful cutting; ideally a spot face cutter tool is used, but a 3.0mm sharp twist drill bit can also be used with care.

A CDU is relatively easy to produce at home. The circuit requires an input diode to ensure that the positive is always correctly presented to the capacitor(s), or use a bridge rectifier and a transistor that can handle the instantaneous discharge current from the capacitor(s). Note the reference to capacitors in the plural, as more than one may be used to allow greater storage capacity and a larger discharge, especially where two or more solenoid motors are to move from one switch operation. The input volts to the CDU can be 16 to 22 volts AC or 22 to 30 volts DC. If a bridge rectifier is used, both AC and DC inputs can be connected either way round to the input terminals. Please be aware that with any electrolytic capacitor circuit the capacitor, once charged, retains that charge for a long time once power is turned off. If working on the circuit, turn off the power and operate a point switch to discharge the capacitor(s) safely.

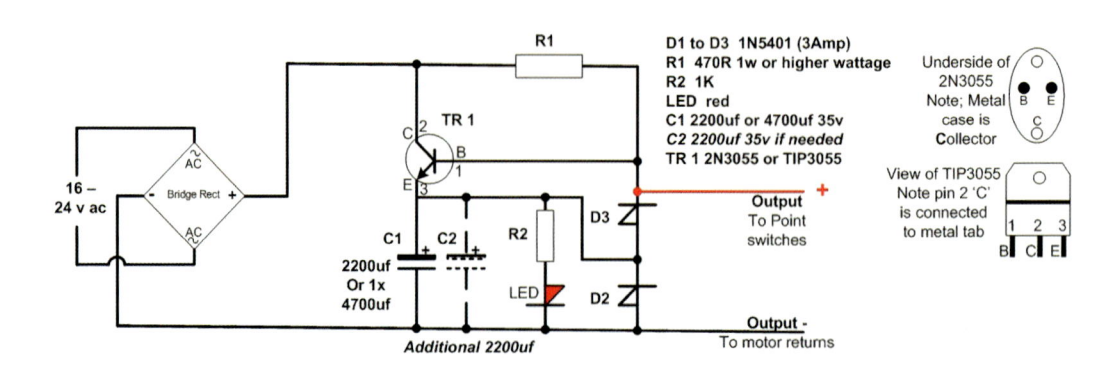

A Capacitor Discharge Unit (CDU) with a bridge rectifier.

PIC micro-controllers

These little Integrated Circuits (ICs) are programmable and can be used over and over again for different types of circuit, although the user should obtain the best Peripheral Interface Controller (PIC) for the job it is required for. A PIC programming board is almost an essential part of the setting-up process, and I have found using a software programme like PICAXE makes the understanding, testing and final downloading of the finished programme very simple. PICAXE Editor 6 version 6.1 is the latest version at the time of writing, but it is well worth checking for later updates or newer issues, all of which are free. Once the programme is installed on a computer, it is very simple to use, and format operations via flow chart connections makes assembling a circuit, then testing it, simple. No knowledge of BASIC programming is required, although some will enjoy learning BASIC if they don't already have a grasp of it.

Circuits to control traffic lights, infrared train detection, railway signalling, and much more are simple to assemble and use.

Infrared

Mentioning infrared (IR) provides the opportunity to discuss this a little bit more. Infrared sends out invisible light, which is reflected back to an infrared receiver. When the bounced signal is received it causes the receiver to alter state, and that alteration can be used to switch other devices such as a transistor or the input to a PIC or other IC device. The great advantage is that IR does not require any alterations to be made to rolling stock, and works with whatever passes over or in front of its beam. IR transmitters and receiver LEDs are readily available and can cost very little. I personally like the dual-packed RPR220 device, which, once working in a circuit, can simply sit between two OO-scale sleepers in a hole drilled into the baseboard.

In the RPR220 package is a infrared transmitter (Tx) LED and a infrared receiver (Rx) LED (transistor). By feeding the Tx with a constant supply via a suitable series resistor, the infrared light is constantly being emitted. As a item such as a loco or carriage passes over or in front of the device, the infrared beam is reflected off it and the Rx then 'sees' the infrared and causes the circuit to which it is connected to operate. While to the human eye the infrared LED cannot be seen to be lit, if a camera, such as one built into a cell phone, is used, the pinkish colour of the lit infrared LED can clearly be seen.

By designing the PIC micro-controller to carry out various functions, when one of its input pins is triggered the outputs can directly turn on or off via a suitable series resistor one LED such as a signal aspect. Note that the outputs of a PIC are relatively low current rated and, while they can easily feed a single LED, any larger current that needs to be switched should be via a transistor fed from the output. Where a relay is switched, always add an inverse diode across the relay coil to remove the back electro-motive force (EMF) created as the coil is turned off, as this can easily damage the transistor.

When using any electronics, and you are switching a supply to a input pin, always connect the pin via typically a 10K resistor to either the positive supply (VCC) or the negative (0 volts), then the switch to the other supply rail. This then biases the pin, ensuring that it will not operate randomly and will only operate as intended when the switch closes or opens. This is called 'pull up' or 'pull down'.

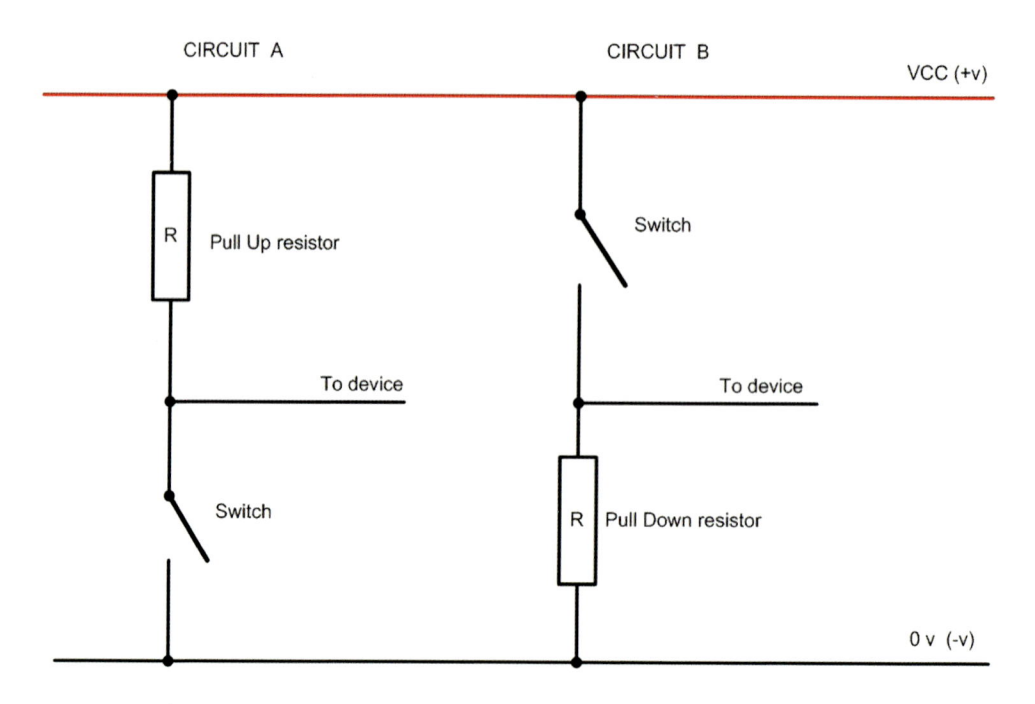

This diagram shows the basic idea of biasing the input for both states VCC or 0. In the left-hand example Circuit A is a pull-up and the 'device' receives VCC all the while that the switch is open. When it closes, the 'device' is connected to 0 volts. The opposite occurs in Circuit B, where the 'device' is connected to 0 volts all the while that the switch is open via the resistor. When the switch closes, VCC appears to the 'device'. The 'device' can be anything required, e.g. a micro-controller's input pin or a transistor base, etc The value of R can be whatever is required, but frequently 10K or more is used.

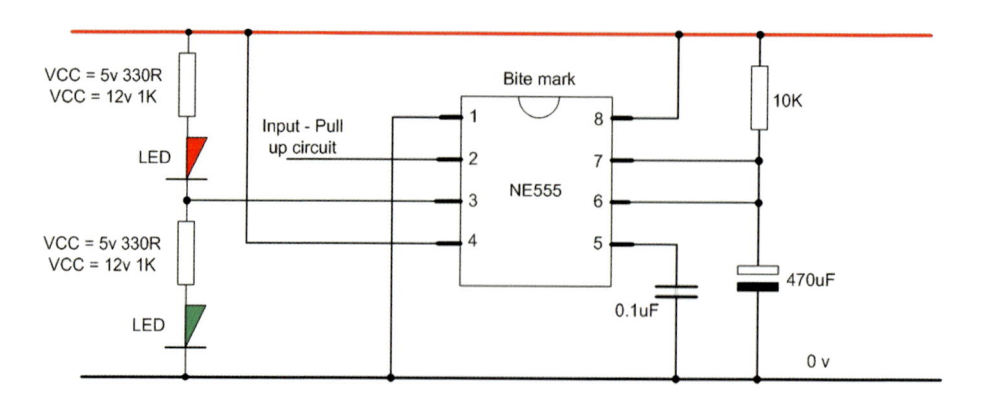

In this simplistic diagram, using an NE555 IC, it can be seen how, depending on the IC's input setting (high or low) on pin 2, an LED can be controlled, which will time for a preset period once the switch is opened. The timing period is determined by the value of the resistor and electrolytic capacitor on pins 6 and 7. Use Circuit A (pull up) for the input, then try Circuit B (pull down). Values of resistors for the LEDs will need to be calculated and will depend on VCC supply volts and the LEDs' forward voltage rating. The diagram is shown purely as an example and not necessarily as a working prototype, although it will work as shown with the correct component values. The two LEDs with their series resistors are connected to the IC's single output pin, then one LED will light when the output is positive and the other when it is negative (0 or 1 state).

11
Lineside detailing

Lineside detailing includes the boundary fence, telegraph poles, cable routes, point rodding and everything else 'railway'.

Fencing

UK railways fence in all the railway to prevent easy access, something not found in many European countries or in the Americas. Fencing comes in many styles from five-stranded open wire and post to chain link or palisade wooden fencing through to metal fencing. Its purpose is to keep animals and trespassers off the railway, so its style is very much dependant on what it is to be used for. In country areas five-strand wire fencing is the norm. This simple fencing often has concrete posts and five single-stranded wires running between them, and is a cheap option where human trespass is not a problem. It is still frequently used, but not ideal where sheep or other livestock are occupying the field adjacent to the railway; sheep tend to get between the strands and are able to then gain access to the running line or lineside areas where the grass is always greener!

Five-wire fencing can be modelled by using proprietary plastic moulded posts and fine nylon line or fishing line to represent the strands of wire. Posts can be made from matchsticks or strips of small square-section wood, balsa or plastic strip. When positioned in fine pre-drilled holes and the posts glued in place, they make a good representation of the real thing.

Chain link fencing is used in more urban areas where human trespass is likely. It can vary in height and may even have a strand or two of barbed wire on the top. It is harder to reproduce, but the use of an open-weave material such as that used in the plastering trade for bridging plasterboard joints makes a good representation. Posts for the model fence are again made from wood or plastic and are frequently coloured to represent concrete.

Palisade fencing is frequently used on platforms in country areas and along the sides of level crossings of both the gated and barrier form. It is much more involved to make and perhaps the best option is to use one of the many commercial styles produced in plastic. This can be painted in the railway company's colours on platforms or white at level crossings. Palisade can be upright struts spaced roughly one strut apart, or angled to around 45 degrees and at times also interlaced with struts going in the opposite 45-degree angle.

Anti-climb steel fencing is used mainly to protect industrial sites or railway workshop areas, where trespass and theft is likely. Some have a curved top, while other styles are straight bars with spiked tops. I haven't tried to reproduce this style, and believe it may be quite hard and tedious to undertake! Commercially produced anti-climb fencing is available in most scales.

Telegraph poles

These are usually associated with railways that represent the pre-1970s era, but examples can still be found on some UK railway lines, especially in rural areas. The telegraph pole is or was used to transmit telephone signals and signalling circuits on open copper wires, although towards the latter part of their life the copper wire was often covered in a PVC jacket.

Telegraph poles were placed clear of the running line and normally on the inside of a curve. They had 'arms' at the top that carried insulated ceramic (usually china) pots to which the wires were attached. How many arms and pots used on the post depended on the area and type of line; a main-line telegraph pole might have ten or more arms each with four pots/wires on each side of the post, while on more rural lines it might only have a couple of arms and four pots/wires per arm.

Pole circuits were used for block bell and block section control from signal box to signal box, as well as telephone circuits. In addition, it was not unusual to have some wires used for actual signalling purposes, especially for distant signals where an electric indication confirming the signal's aspect was sent back to the controlling signal box, also indicating whether or not the signal was lit correctly. Some wires carried a higher voltage of 110 volts, usually on red-coloured pots, and this was used to charge batteries located at distant signals.

Some poles had double arms fitted, the arms being adjacent on either side of the post, while others had just single arms on one side of the post. It is recorded that where single arms were used they were normally fitted to the side of the pole that was closer to London! Double-armed poles often had transposition crossovers in their wire circuits to overcome the possibility of induced noise and cross talk. Here a top pair of wires were transposed by jumpers to lower arms and were often also twisted around to make the upper left wire become the lower right one, etc.

Tall poles were produced to allow the wires to pass over roads or across the railway. Poles and their wires were installed so that a minimum clearance was achieved; over the railway the minimum clearance was deemed to be 17 feet above rail top. At rural farm crossings, 16 feet above the road surface was the norm, and when passing over a main road the lowest wire would be at least 20 feet above the road.

Poles were stayed on curves to stop them being pulled in towards the curve, and also stayed at termination posts to act against the natural pull of the wires. Stays were made of twisted galvanised wire, the galvanised coating helping to prevent rusting. More than one stay might be used to help support a post. Generally, telegraph poles were spaced 60 to 65 yards apart, but became closer on curves. In 4mm scale, 60 yards (180 feet) is equal to 720mm, which would probably not look correct, so compression is used. In OO 4mm/foot, a pole spacing of around 400-450mm seems to look about right, but of course spacings can be increased as wished.

Posts usually had a cap on top made of

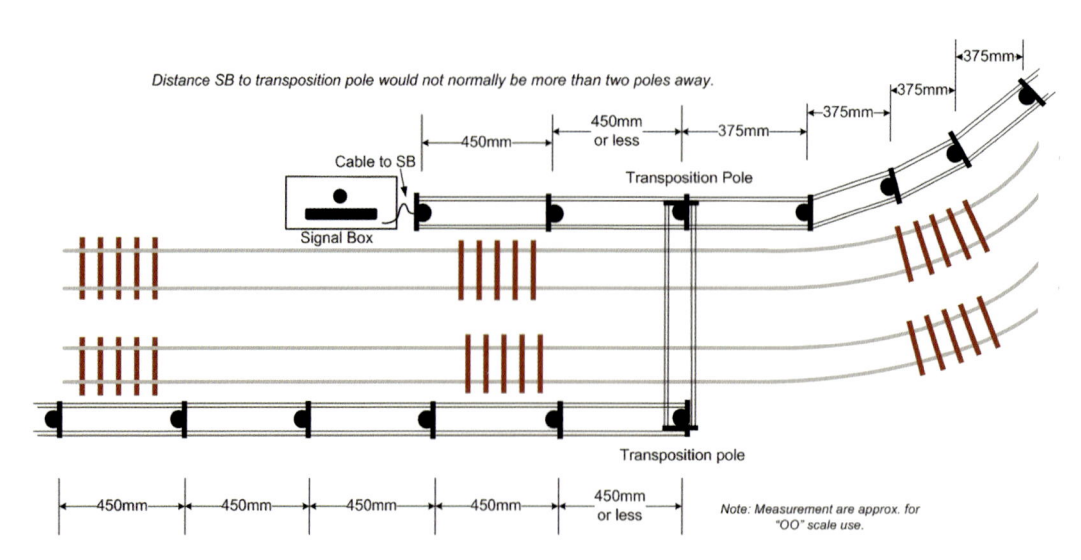

An aerial view of a typical pole route.

galvanised zinc or lead in a sort of inverted V shape. This helped to prevent premature rot at the top of the pole. Pole steps were normally fitted from around 10-12 feet above ground to just below the lowest arm, and these generally alternated on each side of the pole; quite often the last top step also had a diagonally mating step to allow the linesman to stand on the top pair of steps while working on lower wires.

A typical lineside telegraph. *Courtesy of www.1900s.org.uk*

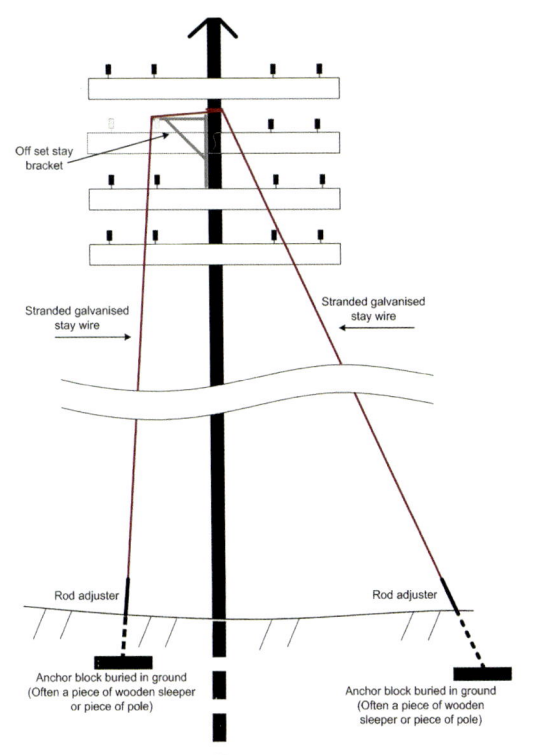

A model telegraph pole set next to a tunnel portal on an OO-scale layout.

Goods yards

Yard lights can be either on wooden poles (such as telegraph poles) or on concrete or steel posts. They are used to provide footpath lighting for loco crews and shunters, etc, and were originally lit be either oil or gas. More modern ones will use filament lamps and the latest possibly high-powered flood lighting from large tungsten filament lamps, mercury vapour tubes or, most recently, banks of high-brightness power-saving LEDs. There are several makes of ready-made yard and station lights in all scales, and you can also buy kits to make them. With some skill, home-made yard lamps can be produced from plastic or brass tubing or rodding of a suitably size, and the shade fashioned from a small washer fitted over an LED. The rod and washer can be painted to suit, then 'planted' in a hole drilled in the baseboard and wired to a low-voltage DC power supply.

Tower-style yard floodlights are more difficult to make at home, so perhaps a ready-made item might be the more cost-effective solution. However, if you feel like the challenge, use brass or plastic L- and H-shaped sections with fine flat sections used for other areas.

The use of white or warm white LEDs is ideal for all types of lighting, as they run virtually cold. But do ensure that you add a series current limiting resistor in the LED feed line unless the LED is produced as working at the voltage being used, e.g. a 12-volt LED on a 12-volt DC supply. Otherwise use a 610- to 1,000-ohm (610R to 1K0) series resistor on 12 volts DC. Increase the resistor's ohm value to dim the LED. I have found warm white LEDs offer a light similar to filament (tungsten) lighting, while white LEDs are more likely to represent fluorescent or high-powered LED outside lighting.

Lineside buildings

Permanent way (p.way) huts were used by the track length gangs until BR modernised track maintenance and used mobile track gangs. P.way huts were placed along the trackside at intervals of roughly 2 to 4 miles, although they could be closer or further apart depending on locality. They were the 'base camp' for the gang of men who maintained a specific length of track, hence the term 'length gangs'. The gangs were often six to eight men strong, and a chargehand called a 'ganger' took overall responsibility for the track section and his men. The hut provided them with shelter, a place to sit and eat their food, store their tools and other equipment, as well as a place where the ganger could do his office duties – daily time sheets and work completed sheets, etc. The hut frequently had a brick-built chimney and hearth where the 'tea boy' would heat hot water for the gang's brew at lunchtime, and possibly more often on a wet day.

Many huts were built from wooden sleepers with a tar or pitch covered roof, a dirt floor and a long wooden table with two benches each side, with possibly a further bench along a wall. The ganger had a high-legged chair and a tall Dickensian-style writing desk. No one was normally allowed to use this chair and desk except the ganger or someone he nominated! The gangs were fiercely competitive of each other and used to keep their track section in tiptop condition. In my very early days on the railway I saw ballast stones aligned in a neat row along the edge of the ballast shoulder where it met the flat outer cess area. The gangs were well known for riding their bicycles along the cess to reach their section and hut. Modelling of the flat, narrow cess area should be carried out wherever possible.

P.way huts are readily available pre-built and painted in all scales or as kits in plastic, laser-cut wood or card. They could of course

A typical Southern Region concrete p.way hut, now dilapidated and unused. Courtesy of Tony Strickland

also be made from card and printed paper, or even produced from plastic embossed sheets and scrap box items.

Another hut often seen on pre-modernisation railways was often located at a distant signals, or possibly positioned at other strategic signals, and this was the 'fogging hut'. They were smaller than p.way huts and were normally a one-man unit, much like a sentry box, and were used by operations or, more frequently, trained p.way staff for fogging and falling snow duties. During fog (smog too) and falling snow, the railway operators would send a trained person to just beyond the distant or other signal, and they were instructed to place one detonator on the running rail on the approach side of the signal when the signal was 'on' (at caution or danger). The train would run over the detonator producing a very loud bang, and the train driver was instantly made aware of the approaching invisible signal being 'on'. The detonator was then replaced with a fresh one pending the arrival of the next train all the while the signal remained 'on'. The hut provided some basic shelter for the fogman and also provided some protection from the flying shrapnel from the exploding detonators. Quite often a small brazier for holding an open fire would be located at the hut. Again, ready-made or kit-built items are available, and home-made huts are fairly easy to construct.

Goods sheds

Goods sheds were used predominantly up until the mid-1960s to load and unload produce and materials that came from or were going to local businesses. After this time most goods were sent by road rather than rail, as Dr Beeching's cuts closed many smaller lines where such sheds would have been in daily use.

The typical goods shed offered a covered area with a single track running inside along one side of the building, and usually a raised platform abutted the track. The shed helped keep the goods being loaded or unloaded dry. Wagons would be pushed or pulled into the shed and left there for the local goods staff to load or unload, then when ready the wagon was taken away to the main sidings for assembly into a goods train ready to go out onto the main line and its final destination. The road side of the goods shed had access to the raised platform to aid moving the goods from vehicle to platform. Heavy items would be moved by a small hand-operated crane located inside or outside the shed on a platform of its own. Models of goods sheds are available in all scales, either ready built or in kit form. There are some lovely examples available in assorted finishes to represent brick or stone, and even wood.

A similar shed, known as a 'provender store', was also used by some regions and these generally held goods such as grain, cattle food and other produce. They were usually raised off the ground on short stilts of brick or concrete pillars. Many provender stores were made of pre-fabricated concrete slabs. There are several kits and ready-made examples available for the modeller.

Signal boxes

Signal boxes are the control centre of the railway, in which one or more signallers operate levers or panel buttons, or today use computer screens and keyboards to control train movements. Early signal boxes usually had the signaller and signalling equipment at least one level above ground. Some were built much higher, or even spanned the tracks. This raised position provided the signaller with a better view of approaching and passing trains, while all the mechanical interlocking, signal wires and point rodding were housed in the area below the signaller's floor, affording good access to this equipment for the signal maintenance staff.

Some signal boxes were located at ground level, and these were often found at level crossings, controlling both crossing protection signals and the crossing gates; some were located on the station platform. Many signal boxes where constructed either from all wood or the lower portion of brick and the upper portion wood. Later signal boxes where mainly all-electric signalling panels are installed were built from all brick or other suitable solid building materials.

Today's high-tech signalling centres are

largely made from steel framing with suitable cladding applied to the frames. IECCs (Integrated Electronic Control Centres) house work stations containing computer screens and keyboards and have several signallers operating individual large sections of the railway, the whole IECC being responsible for controlling many hundreds of track miles. Most IECCs have fully automatic computer-controlled route setting and signalling and the signaller only needs to take over control in the event of a problem occurring that the computer is unable to deal with.

Point rodding is used where mechanically operated points are operated from levers in the signal box. Early installations used a round rod, while later installations, or where the old rod run has been upgraded, used inverted U-channel made of galvanised steel. Whichever type is modelled it is fairly easy to represent using plastic tubing, plastic square or U-section, and kits are also available for most gauges. The harder parts to

Both types of point rodding can be seen here on the 'real' railway. Lower right is newer galvanised U-shaped channel rodding which is connecting to older round rodding in the middle to upper left.

In the foreground is the non-working OO scale Wills SS89 point rodding kit made up to represent rodding leading away from a signal box. An extension kit, SS90, is also available to further enhance the rod run. *Courtesy of Railway Modeller/PECO*

make yourself are the right-angle cranks that were used to change the rodding's direction from the main rod run to the actual point. There are some smaller manufacturers who produce brass etch items for producing your own rod runs and these include cranks and compensator cranks, all found in conventional rod runs. A well-laid model from the signal box to all points looks great, but does take a lot of planning and care when installing the runs. Easier to use is the plastic non-working point rodding such as the Wills SS89 kit, but this is currently only available in OO scale.

Concrete cable ducting, or 'troughing', is seen everywhere on the modern railway and carries signalling cables, telecommunication cables and, where the line is electrified, traction power cables. High-voltage power cables used for traction are kept separate and their own route is frequently on the opposite side of the railway or, where space is limited, the two troughings run alongside each other. This ducting is usually made of concrete in various widths and heights. The main body is U-shaped, into which the cables are laid and a separate flat concrete lid fits on top to provide a fully covered cable enclosure.

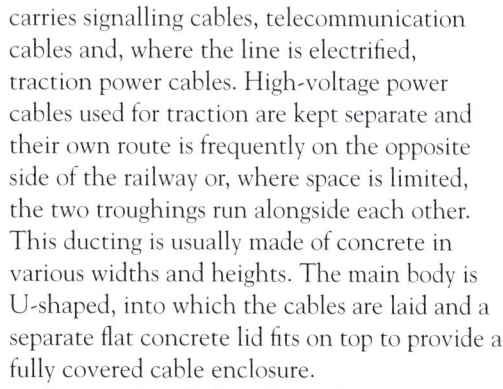

Frequently a T-shaped trough is inserted in the run where cables in the troughing enter and leave lineside apparatus cabinets. These mainly contain signalling items, such as track circuit feed and relay end equipment, axle counter components and signalling controls, either via relays or electronic modules, together with rows of terminals to which the cables are connected. Telecoms cabinets are usually smaller but are still fed by T-shaped troughing.

A typical lineside concrete troughing cable route with, nearest the camera, the lids in place. This ducting can be simply modelled by using either rectangular or inverted U-section plastic with the top surface scored to represent the gaps between lids. Troughing lids are generally 36 inches or 1 metre long – around 12mm spacing in OO scale. Commercially made kits are also available. *Courtesy of Adrian Lee*

12
Railway signalling

Semaphore signalling

Originally trains were dispatched from place 'A' and expected to arrive at place 'B' within a certain time limit. Once this set time had elapsed, a second train could be dispatched from A and was expected to arrive at B. All this worked well until the first train didn't arrive at B inside the expected time frame; anything could have caused it to be delayed or stopped between A and B. The second train, having been dispatched, proceeded and eventually found the first train sitting in its path. Results could be catastrophic!

Clearly some form of communication between A and B and vice versa was needed. Thus the telegraph system was developed and the signaller at A could advise the signaller at B that a train had left and B could then tell A that it had arrived and A could then dispatch another train safe in the knowledge that the line ahead was clear. From this simple system 'block working' evolved, and visible indicators were used to remind the signaller of the presence of a train and also lock the exit signals, preventing accidental clearing of a signal to allow the passage of a train before the section between the two signal boxes was clear. This system is still in use in some areas today but is generally on the decline where resignalling works are undertaken.

While I mention specific styles of BR signals, there are regional variations and it becomes impossible to include every variant. These descriptions are general, and if you are modelling a specific region and time period the best option is to research that era and location from dedicated books or the Internet.

The signalling of a train evolved from the basic signalman (sometimes called a 'bobby') standing with a red flag to a signaller working in a specially built cabin, or signal box. In the box were levers used to operate the signals and points remotely. Eventually levers were mechanically interlocked to stop conflicting moves being made. Later the mechanical interlocking was improved by electrical lever locks, adding to the protection of trains.

The signal levers are usually painted red for stop signals and yellow for distant signals. The lever, which is either straight or L-shaped, pivots at over half way along its length, and for the L-shaped lever the pivot is at the right-angle. The lever frequently had a chain connected to its end and this was taken via pulley wheels to where it eventually connected to a multi-strand wire, which led away to where the signal was located via right-angled cranks and pulley wheels. The movement of the lever allowed the signal arm to be moved to the proceed ('off') position, giving the train driver a good and clear indication that he could proceed. This formed the basics of semaphore railway signalling.

Two types of semaphore signals were used, upper quadrant and lower quadrant. Both types had the signal arm in the horizontal position for stop (when the signal is 'on'). The upper quadrant arm moved from the horizontal to around 45 degrees above horizontal to give a proceed ('off') indication to the driver, while the lower quadrant arm dropped below horizontal by approximately 45 degrees to give the proceed aspect. The two styles are very rarely ever intermixed; a whole section or region would usually have one type of semaphore signal. If the wire to the arm broke while the arm was 'off', the natural weight of the arm and counter weights would return the arm to the 'on' position, so the system was fail safe in the main. Of course, it was not unknown occasionally for the arm not to return to 'on' for some reason, possibly due to ice or snow holding the arm 'off', which resulted in a 'wrong side' signalling failure, an extremely serious event.

When facing an approaching train the signal arm was painted red with a white vertical band towards its outer end; the reverse side of the arm was white with a black horizontal band in line with the front white band. Glasses or spectacles, called 'specs', were fitted to the pivot end of the signal arm; one was red and the other green (the green had a distinct blue shade that, when combined with the yellowish flame of the illuminating oil lamp, produced a better green colour). Originally a paraffin oil lamp was used to illuminate the spectacles, which had a clear glass domed lens that the flame was adjusted to show through. The lamps were for night use and offered a somewhat poor level of illumination, but were used for many years. Today semaphore signals tend to have electric lamps for night-time use, though there are still some areas using paraffin oil lamps!

Where the signal is positioned out of view of the signaller in the signal box an arm position indicator is used, which is electrically operated and shows the signaller what the actual signal arm is displaying to the driver by means of a swinging arm indicator, usually mounted above the lever controlling that signal. These indicators show 'Off', 'On' or 'Wrong', 'Wrong' indicating that the arm isn't fully 'off' or 'on'; they normally have a white dial face with a red or black pointer.

A 'lamp lit' indicator could also be found for signals not seen directly by the signaller. These were used for signals lit by oil lamps and were simple bi-metal strips, and the heat of the paraffin lamp's flame caused the strip to bend and make a contact. If the lamp went out the bi-metal cooled and broke the contact, and the indicator in the signal box showed 'Out'.

Long wire runs from the signal box to the signal frequently had ratchet-style wire adjusters in the signal box, which allowed the signaller to slacken or tension the wire as required due to temperature changes. Some long wire runs incorporated weighted compensators to allow for semi-automatic wire tensioning; these also helped the signaller somewhat with the heavy load placed on the lever and the hard pull required to move it over to operate the signal.

As well as the red 'stop' signal there was the 'distant' signal. If this was 'off' it indicated to the train driver that the section of signalling ahead had all signals cleared to proceed; if 'on' – horizontal, the signal could be passed but warned the driver that the next signal was 'on', or the whole route ahead hadn't been cleared to proceed. The distant signal arm was also either upper or lower quadrant style and differed from the stop arm in that the arm was yellow facing the oncoming train with a 'fishtail' V-shape cut into the outer end. There was a black V-shaped band on the front of the arm a little way in from the end. The reverse of the distant arm was usually all white with a black V-shaped band matching the front black one. There was generally one distant signal for each direction or route approaching the signalling section. As with the stop signal, the distant had two spectacles that were lit during the hours of darkness, but showed yellow when 'on' and green when 'off'. On the approach to junctions two or more distant arms indicated which route ahead had been selected and whether the whole section for that route was clear or not. The distant signal levers in the signal box were usually at the outer ends of the row of red levers and were painted yellow. Note that the distant arm could not be cleared to 'off' until all signals in that route ahead were also cleared.

Distant signals were generally placed at least about half a mile before the stop signal, and exceptionally long wire runs of a mile or more were not unusual. Later years saw the advent of the motorised mechanical distant signal, whereby an electric motor was operated by the lever in the signal box and the motor in turn powered the signal arm to the 'off' position; on removing the power the arm returned to 'on' by the weight of the counter balance. Indications of the position of the arm was again relayed back to the signal box, with a swinging arm position indicator normally over the controlling lever; this indicator usually had a black dial face and a white or yellow pointer.

Main-line junctions were signalled using multiple posts and arms bracketed on one main post, the posts arranged side by side in a 'stepping' arrangement. The main-line route was signalled by the taller post and diverging lines by lower posts arranged to the left or right of the main post depending on which way the lines diverged from the main line. Where arms were placed one above the other on the same post, usually on sidings or goods lines, this was called 'stacking'. Where a bracketed signal had the arms at the same height, each diverging line was considered to be as important as the other.

In our model form signalling can be of either type – semaphore or colour light (see below). However, don't intermix them, except if a colour light distant is combined with semaphore signalling.

Semaphores and colour light signals can be purchased ready-made, in kit form or built from scratch. Semaphores can be operated mechanically via fine line (fishing line is often used) from a lever frame. Alternatively they can be electrically operated via solenoid coils, stepper motors or servos, or just left fixed in the 'off' or 'on' position as required.

Currently Dapol produces a working semaphore signal of various styles in OO and 'N' scale. These are 'planted' into a hole drilled in the baseboard and wired to a simple press-to-make push button or switch and of course to a suitable power supply. At the time of writing there are no off-the-shelf working semaphore signals for other scales, although there are a small number of specialist manufacturers that can undertake orders for working signals. Older modellers may recall the Hornby Dublo working semaphore signals, which at times

The two red and white banded signals are stop signals, one for each line, and are protecting the entrance to the single track beyond. In the distance is the rear view of a bracket signal. The rear of each arm is white with a black band. Each arm protects the line where it diverges into two tracks; the right-hand arm as seen by an approaching train would control moves into the right-hand line, while the left-hand arm controls moves onto the left-hand line.

can still be found second-hand, but their size is rather over-scale for OO railways and are somewhat toy-like in their appearance.

Colour light signals

Colour light signals first appeared around the early 1930s and slowly progressed around British Railways, replacing semaphore signalling. They could be intermixed with semaphores and one of the most common examples is a colour light distant signal in an otherwise totally semaphore section.

A colour light distant signal would only show a yellow or green aspect. In early days they were battery powered from lead acid cells fitted in the cabinet at the base of the signal, and charging of the batteries was via dedicated pole route wires that carried nominally 110 volts to the signal from a local power supply input cabinet, often at the signal box. The batteries ensured that the signal was always lit, even when power outages were experienced. The aspects of the colour light distant on the approach to a semaphore signalled section are exactly as per the semaphore distant signal, in that the green aspect could only be illuminated if the whole section ahead was all clear, otherwise the distant remained at yellow.

Two-aspect signalling is used where train traffic is exceptional light, typically on branch lines or lines where train density is low. Such signals display red or green, red and yellow, or yellow and green depending on their position in the signalling area. Three-aspect signalling is used where train density is greater, the line speed is frequently lower, and braking and stopping distances are longer between signals. Three-aspect signals normally display red, yellow or green aspects. In four-aspect signalling – yellow, green, yellow, red from top to bottom – two yellows indicates that the next signal is at yellow and the next but one is at red; green indicates that the section ahead is clear.

All colour light signals are arranged so as the red aspect is closest to the driver's eye-line. Thus, for post- or gantry-mounted signals this will mean that red is the bottom aspect. Where a signal must be ground mounted – normally inside tunnels – the red swaps position to the top, keeping it nearest to the driver's eye-line. So, from bottom up, a tunnel ground-mounted colour light signal would read yellow, green, second yellow if four-aspect, and red at the top.

BR colour light signals used filament lamps to illuminate the aspects. Usually the lamps had twin filaments, and these are employed with one or both filaments illuminated depending on the lamp style in use in that particular signalling area. The idea was that should one filament fail, the other would be able to take over until the lamp could be replaced. More modern signalling now employs LED (Light Emitting Diode) illumination, and as the LEDs can produce three colours in one lens, signal heads are reduced to one lens for the red, yellow and green. Where four-aspect signalling is used a second lens and LED light is fitted above the first and lights only to show a yellow when the second yellow aspect is required, otherwise it stays unlit The use of LED lighting has improved signalling tremendously as it offers virtually fail-free illumination and a much clearer and less ambiguous aspect.

Where a junction is signalled by colour lights, a Junction Route Indicator (JI), also known as a 'feather', is used. This usually sits on top of the main signal head and illuminates with rows of five white lights. There are six positions for UK JIs and each indicates the route to be taken left or right from the main line. The six positions are numbered 1 to 6; position 1 is top left, position 2 middle left and position 3 lower left, while 4 to 6 are top right, middle right and lower right respectively. The upper and lower positions are approximately at 45 degrees to the horizontal. Eckon produces an OO scale JI, but this is only available in position 1 or position 4. Wire the signal via the signal post tube to below the baseboard, then the choice is to use a manual switch to operate it or perhaps have automatic illumination via a point-operated position switch. Here I would be inclined to ensure that the red aspect is not lit when the JI is to become lit; a relay or some form of electronics can be used to prevent this.

Position 1 shows that the route is set for the first track to the left of the main line, position 2 the second track to the left and position 3 the

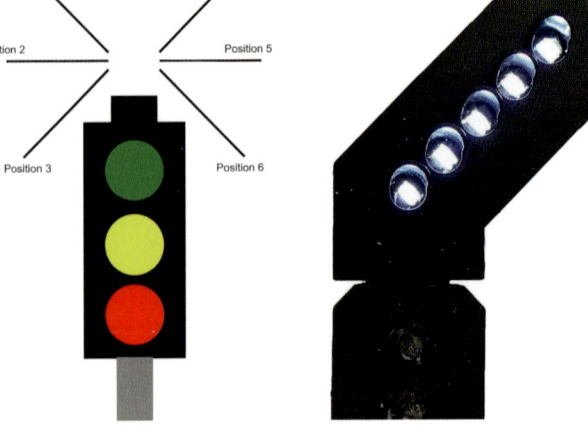

Above: A colour light Junction Indicator.

The left-hand signal shows a position 1 left-hand Junction Indicator, while the right-hand signal head shows position 4 for a right-hand junction. *Courtesy of Train-Tech*

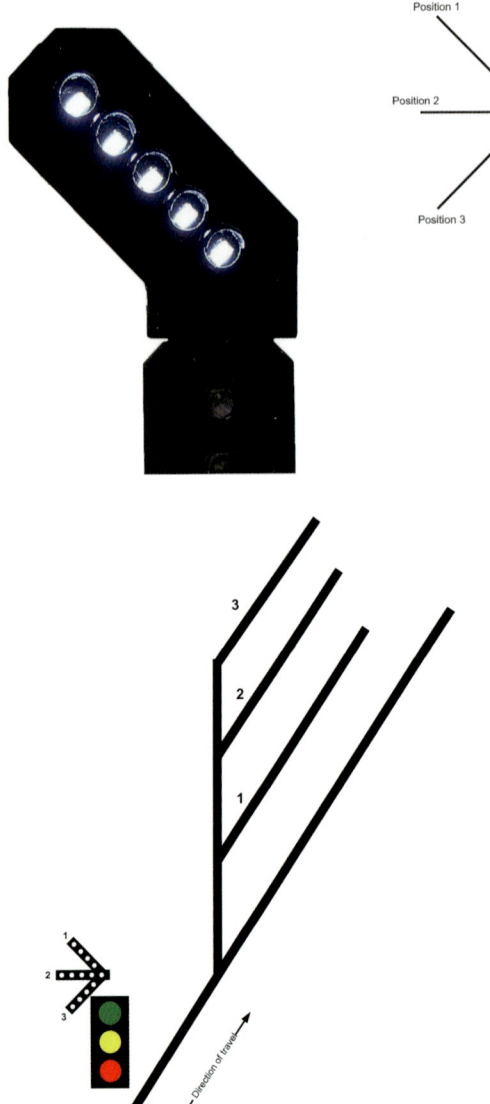

Left: How positions 1 to 3 relate to the diverging routes ahead.

third track over from the main line. Positions 4 to 6 are the same but apply to tracks leading off to the right, with position 4 being the first track over from the main line.

Another means of advising the train driver of the direction to be taken is the use of 'theatre' lights, which illuminate a letter or number relating to a track ahead. Originally these used a dot matrix display of small pigmy lamps, but these have been replaced by LED theatre lights that show white letters or numbers. They are reproduced in the model form mainly by specialist manufacturers such as

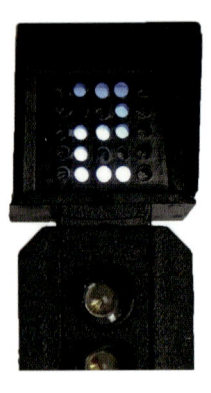

A 'theatre' junction indicator. *Courtesy of Train-Tech*

Absolute Aspects, while home-made units can be produced using commercial small seven-segment LED matrix units. However, obtaining white LED types is a little harder as many of the readily available ones are yellow or other colours such as red or green. But white can be found with a little searching. They need very careful wiring and the use of ultra-fine wires to their pins and onward down the signal post to the underboard connections and finally to the switching to illuminate them. Train-Tech has produced a theatre light for OO that illuminates but can only show one pre-set number or letter, which users set themselves

For the modeller colour light signalling is available in most scales and is produced as both working or non-working signals. Typical examples of OO scale non-working colour light signals are the items produced by Knightwing and Bachmann in the UK. Working colour lights are produced by several manufacturers, and the Eckon and Berko range offer a good choice for the kit-builder. Ready-made ranges of colour light signals are also produced by specialist producers such as Train-Tech, CR Signals and Absolute Aspects, to name but three. In addition, in OO scale there is the Hornby range, which are now LED-lit rather than the filament lamps formerly used. But I find these to be somewhat overscale and toy-like in appearance. Most colour light signals use LEDs as the light source as they offer cool running, good colour rendition and long life if fed correctly with power.

Ground or shunt signals

One other type of signal used is the shunt or ground signal. These are either mechanical disc-style shunt signals or the electrically lit aspect type. Two distinct styles are used, as for main signals. The mechanically operated discs have a horizontal red band on a white background; the disc, known as a 'target', indicates stop when horizontal or proceed when angled to around 45 degrees. There is also the caution type, which uses a white background and a yellow horizontal band, or at times a black background with a yellow band. This can be passed in either the horizontal ('on') position or when angled to 45 degrees ('off'), and are mainly used where shunt moves can proceed along a siding without interfering with the main line. Although called ground signals, they can at times be mounted on posts or signal posts.

The modern version is the illuminated shunt signal, also known as a Position Light Signal (PLS). This has two types. The early version used a white 'pivot' lamp and a red horizontal light to signify stop ('on'); when 'off' the pivot remained lit at white and another white light was lit diagonally at 45 degrees and the red extinguished – thus two diagonal whites were shown for proceed. The latest type, used from around the early to mid-1990s uses LEDs and has the pivot lamp as a dual colour. When 'on' the signal displays two red horizontal lights. When set to proceed ('off') the pivot red changes colour to white and the diagonal white is also illuminated, again producing two white lights at around 45 degrees.

Shunt signals are produced in mechanical form by a few kit manufacturers for the user to assemble and paint, or the electric type ready-made in the two versions. Several manufactures produce these and are easy to install and wire.

* Some very useful information on the various types of UK signalling can be viewed online and downloaded as a PDF file at: https://catalogues.rssb.co.uk/rgs/rulebooks/RS521%20Iss%205.pdf

In the first picture a mechanical shunt signal is shown in the 'on' (stop) position, and in the second in the 'off' (proceed) position.

Two OO versions of a working shunt signal. The top one is a representation of a modern shunt signal where the pivot (right-hand light) changes colour from red to white when the signal is 'off'. The lower one is the older style where the pivot is always white.
Courtesy of Train-Tech

Above: The first picture shows a modern ground signal in the 'on' (stop) position, and the second shows the same signal 'off'. Note that the right-hand white light is lit for both positions and is called the 'pivot'. These electrically lit signals are referred to as Position Light Signals (PLS). Working models of these and the more modern twin red/twin white signals are readily available from several UK suppliers such as Eckon, Train-Tech and DCC Concepts or specialist model signal manufacturers. *Courtesy of Adrian Lee, Bluebell Railway*

The same signal in OO showing its 'off' or proceed aspect with two diagonal white lights. *Courtesy of Train-Tech*

13
Electrification - third rail and OLE

Railway electrification falls into two main areas, 'third rail' (conductor rail) or Overhead Line Equipment (OLE). I am deliberately excluding fourth rail electrification schemes as used on many underground railways, as this book deals with systems seen usually on main lines.

Both styles of electrification can be modelled. Modern image modellers or those wishing to portray the UK's Southern Region from around 1930 to the present day have ample opportunities and will find plenty of documentation about these systems of traction power supply. Merseyrail also uses third rail traction. Conductor rail is available in OO scale from Peco, which produces insulated third rail 'pots' and a Code 60 rail to fit into the pots to represent third and even fourth rail systems. C&L Finescale produces a range of pots, ramp ends and guard boards together with a special gauge to aid pot placement. The Scalefour Society commissioned Exacoscale (now C&L) to produce a range of third rail pots, which were sold to society members or via the society's sales stand at exhibitions, but it is unclear if these components are still available. OLE is available ready to use from Peco, Dapol and Summerfeldt, although the latter has a more continental bias. Summerfeldt OLE is available in N, HO and O scales, while Dapol OLE is produced in both N and OO scales. There are a few small 'cottage industry' manufacturers that produce OLE masts, often in brass etch self-assembly kits.

Third rail

Installing third rail means that the layout really has to be permanent and the track well secured. At the time of writing there is no commercially produced ready-to-use third rail for N gauge, but OO, EM and S4/P4 are well covered by the products mentioned previously.

The use of a pot-drilling template is well worth the cost, as it is necessary to fit a pot to the end of every fourth sleeper. A small 0.8mm-diameter hole is drilled, ideally by means of a template (home-made if necessary), and the required number of pots are slid onto the Code 60 rail. This is aided by filing a slight chamfer in the foot of the rail to allow the pot to slide on more easily. Position them in line with the pre-drilled sleeper-end holes, apply a spot of glue (UHU is ideal) to the spigot and insert it into the sleeper-end hole, threading the remaining pots along carefully and gluing each, then positioning them into the holes. A craft knife blade, a jeweller's flat-blade screwdriver and tweezers are all helpful in fitting the rail.

On curves it is best by far to pre-curve the Code 60 rail to the radius required before trying to thread the pots onto it and assembling on the sleepers; the pre-curving will assist the rail to align. Once laid and the glue has had chance to set, try several third rail locos over the area to ensure that the third rail doesn't cause the loco to be lifted on one side and lose contact with the running rail. One thing I've found when using the Peco system on Code 100 OO track is not to use the spacers, as they raised the third rail a little and caused several steam locos to stop operating due to their outside motion rods fouling the third rail.

Third rail is conventionally installed on the sleeper ends between adjacent tracks, in the space that is known as the 'six foot'. At times it will move over to the outermost edges of the sleepers where required by sub-stations or tighter curves. It is always placed on the six-foot side or the opposite side across the track from platforms for passenger safety. Where pointwork occurs, shorter 'floater' sections of third rail are laid, and these can swap sides to maintain a continuous traction supply to the train or loco. The ramped ends of the rail slope downwards, and on the real thing have shallower pots fitted to the ends of the ramp, allowing the train's pick-up shoe to smoothly glide up onto or off the third rail's top surface. There are very many types of ramp ends, and frequently those used by the modeller are of one style covering all applications.

It is at these ramp ends that most arcing is seen on the real thing, and this can be modelled by the use of a blue or blueish-white small high-brightness LED, operated perhaps by an ultra-small reed switch fitted in the track and a magnet on the train that closes the contact of the reed switch as the train passes over the reed. Then by means of a suitable small electronic circuit and power supply, the LED can be caused to rapidly flicker as if an electrical arc is being produced. The arc LED is hidden between the third rail and the running rail.

Once the third rail positioning has been checked, the Code 60 rail needs to be coloured to a dark brown and black finish. The use of a semi-gloss finish on the rail top can represent the de-icing fluid used on the real rail in wintertime.

Guard boarding – generally of wood, although a plastic version is also used on the real railway – can be fashioned from thin plastic strip or thin balsa strip and painted a deep brown or yellow colour. Paper staples can be fashioned and used as guard board supports. Guard boards are fitted on both sides of the conductor rail in station areas and the approaches to level crossings. Where there is a possibility of public trespass or in areas where rail staff are at risk of falling or tripping, in sidings, etc, they are fitted to the inside (running rail side) of the conductor rails. Conductor rails in open country or rural areas is not usually boarded. A more recent location for additional boarding is under road or pedestrian bridges where vandalism is a nuisance; the throwing of metal items off the bridge causes severe damage to the third rail and the running rail due to the heat generated by the arcing created by the metal short circuiting the running rail to the conductor rail.

Heavy duty cables used for traction supply are connected to the real conductor rail and lead off to link one conductor rail to another or to a sub-station. They are easily represented by using black insulated wire of a suitable insulation thickness.

For information, the third rail on former Southern Region routes is at a nominal 750 volts DC with some minor sections running at a slightly lower voltage.

Fourth rail, for those modelling an

The real thing: third rail installed on the outside of the running rails.

This view shows how the third rail sometimes swaps sides from the cess side to the 'six foot'.

Left: The third rail modelled. Peco conductor rail insulator pots are used to hold the conductor rail in place. This is OO scale and the conductor rail is Code 60. Once in place the rail is painted a dirty brown/black colour.

Above: Real insulator pots. They are normally spaced on every fourth sleeper end. They are white but do quickly discolour, mainly due to de-icing fluid being sprayed on them.
Courtesy of Graham Church

This picture shows two different styles of conductor rail ramp ends. In the model form bending the last inch or so of the rail downwards will normally suffice. *Courtesy of Graham Church*

Underground railway line, can be added by the same methods as described for third rail installation. If using the Peco insulating pots, I would recommend not fitting the spacers to the pot's spigot. Fourth rail is installed exactly between the two running rails.

Overhead Line Equipment (OLE)

Overhead Line Equipment (OLE) is the preferred electrification method in the UK today. It was not used on BR's Southern Region main lines, as some of the system had already been laid to third rail before the outbreak of the Second World War, so it was considered more economical to continue the third rail programme into the late 1950s and beyond. The other factor was that tunnels and bridges did not have to be raised to provide the extra clearance that would be needed for OLE.

UK OLE is now standardised at 25,000 volts AC (25KV). For a short time the Southern Region used 750-volt DC OLE in sidings where it was deemed to be hazardous to install the third rail. This system was quickly removed once main-line diesel locomotive traction was used, and much of the 750-volt OLE was taken down and the masts reduced to nothing more than a flush cut-off tube in a concrete ground fitting! A small amount of 1,500-volt DC OLE was used between London, Colchester and Southend on the former Eastern Region and in the north of England (the Woodhead route), but has now been removed. This system mainly used a gantry (portal) supporting system rather than the single mast/post type.

Electrification of the UK rail network is a slow process, with many areas still to be electrified and currently operated by diesel-powered trains. Where electrification has taken place, the contact wire is supported by what is known as the catenary (the whole lot is also known locally as 'the knitting'!), and this is supported on usually galvanised steel masts with arms at right-angles and registration arms holding the main contact wire in either a 'pull off' or 'pull on' mode to provide a zigzag course. Insulators keep the mast and support arm electrically isolated from the main catenary and contact wire. Today, masts are positioned around 50 metres apart, but become closer together on curves.

On multi-track configurations an OLE gantry spans the lines and has several arms supporting the wires above each track. All the wires are held under tension by strategically placed weights located at the ends of the wires. These weights allow the contact wire tension to be maintained due to expansion and contraction in the wire. On the outsides of the masts at high level are generally one or two other wires, and these carry the power and, where a second wire is seen, an electrical return.

The locos and trains have wiper contacts fitted to their roofs, known as 'pantographs', and their contact arm rubs on the underside of the wire and takes the 25KV power down and into the loco or train where it is used to turn the traction motors and provide train heating and lighting, etc. The contact wire zigzags slightly above the track's centre line to prevent wearing a ridge in the pantograph. The contact wire on a UK Mark 3 OLE installation is at 4.7 metres above rail top, although this height will often vary at level crossings, overbridges and depots.

In model form, frequently OLE masts and wires are installed but are not operational, just a dummy system to represent the real thing. Trains run with the pantographs raised and look as though they are picking up power, but are in fact still using the conventional two-rail power supply. However, catenary systems can be made to carry power and if the loco's pantograph is able to collect the power the system can be used separately from the two running rails. On DC layouts this offers the ability to run two trains on the same rails, with one using the two running rails for power, and the other using the OLE and one running rail. This is in fact a common return wiring method. It is not recommended to mix the two methods for DCC. Unfortunately, many ready-made locos fitted with pantographs are non-operational and to convert them would need a lot of skill and work together with the electrical wiring to the motor. It is in my view better to have dummy OLE if it is required.

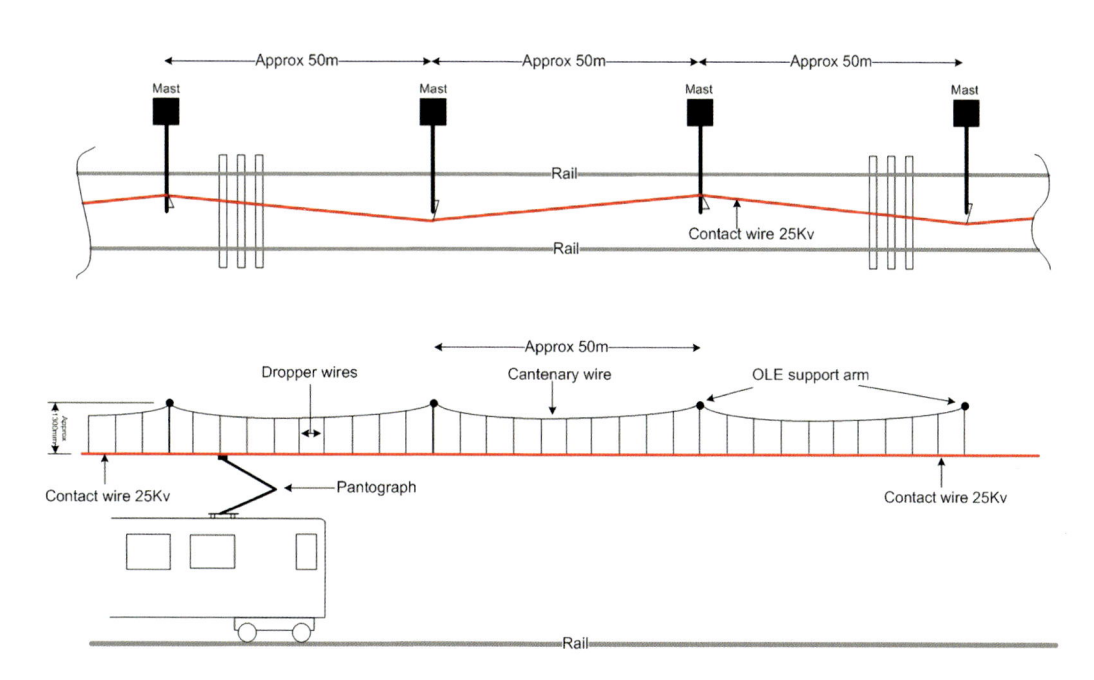

A typical OLE arrangement, showing how the contact wire zigzags.

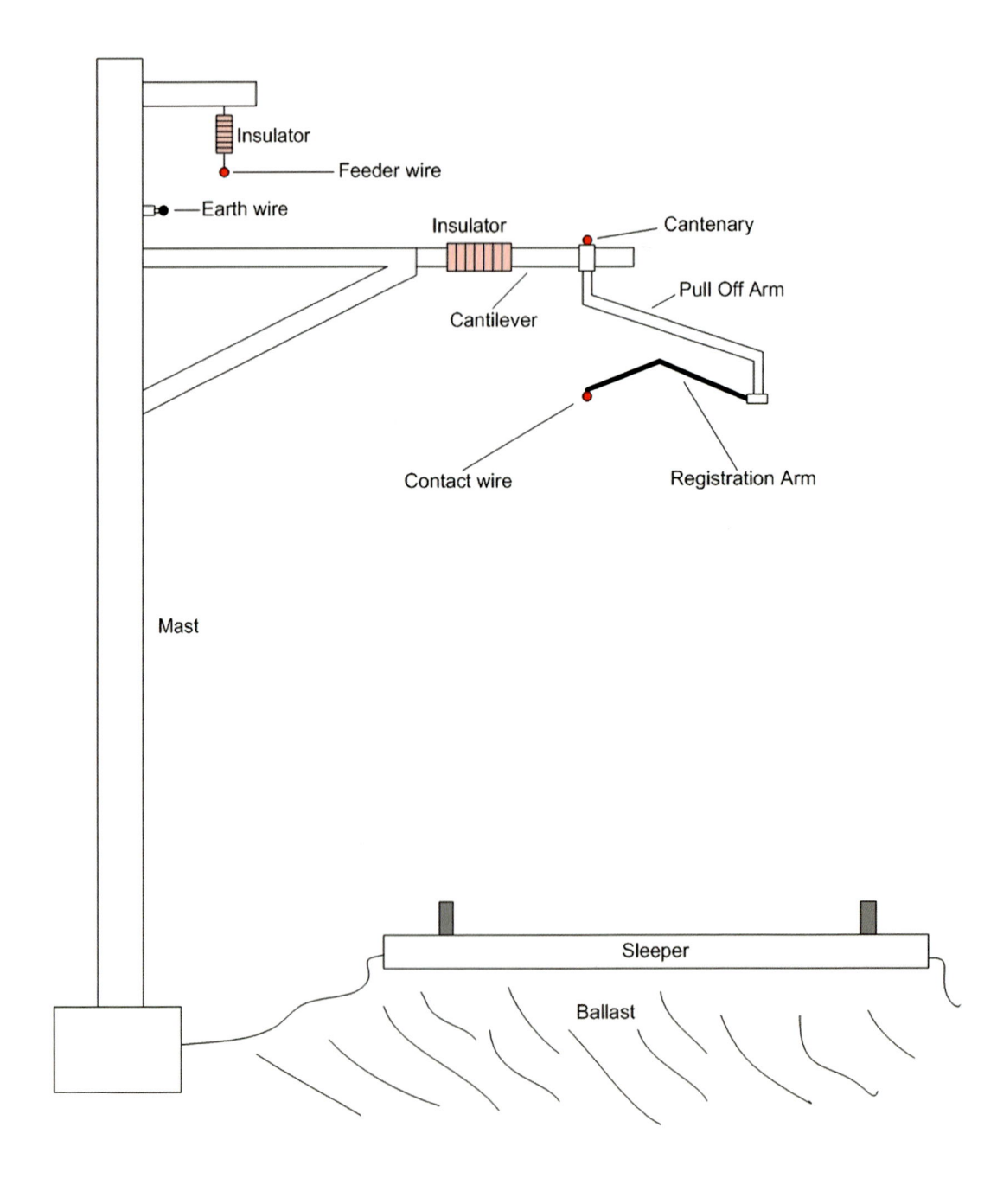

A typical layout drawing of an OLE mast. There are many variations.

Electrification - third rail and OLE

The real thing. Note that the mast furthest from the camera has wire-tensioning weights and pulleys, and that the added mast-side supports counteract the pull of the wires, especially at the ends of wire runs where the weights are fitted.

Left: A close-up view of the contact wire and registration arm.

Peco OLE on an OO layout.
Courtesy of Peco

When installing OLE, a few things should be remembered. If your track is lifted above baseboard level on, say, cork strips or foam underlay, the mast bases need to be raised by the same thickness to keep the contact wire at the correct height – without this added lift it could become too low, causing the pantograph to fold down under its own spring.

Where the OLE goes off scene into a tunnel or siding, etc, and the OLE is not required in these locations, an upward 'ramp' will be needed to allow the pantograph to lift, then at the other end a downward ramp is required to press down the pantograph to its correct height before appearing on the scenic side of the layout. A ramp can be fashioned from Code 55 rail or similar, or a slightly thicker contact wire. A rough idea of the angle of the slope would be around 10 degrees from the scenic-side OLE upwards and downwards to the wire's correct height on exiting the siding or tunnel back to the OLE height.

One thing to remember if installing OLE is that it means rail cleaning becomes much harder where manual rail cleaning is used, as the wires cause a problem in getting a hand under them to allow cleaning, which is an essential job to be regularly undertaken. Thought therefore needs to be given to how rails will be cleaned where the catenary is installed. Consider using a rail cleaning wagon pulled or pushed by a large heavy loco, with its cleaning pad dampened by Isopropyl Alcohol (IPA), methylated spirit (meths) or other proprietary rail-cleaning fluid. Alternatively use a long-arm cleaning tool with a fixed track rubber fitted to its end or a suitable pad that can be moistened with rail cleaner fluid.

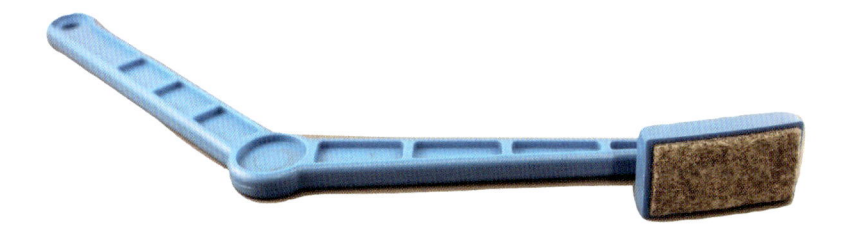

A manual track cleaning pad that can be dampened with fluid such as Isopropyl Alcohol or a proprietary track-cleaning fluid and pushed along the rail tops. This is idea for use on models where access is restricted such as under OLE.

Alternative rail-cleaning methods: a liquid sold with an applicator.

A more conventional 'track rubber' block. *Courtesy of Model Railroad Magazine*

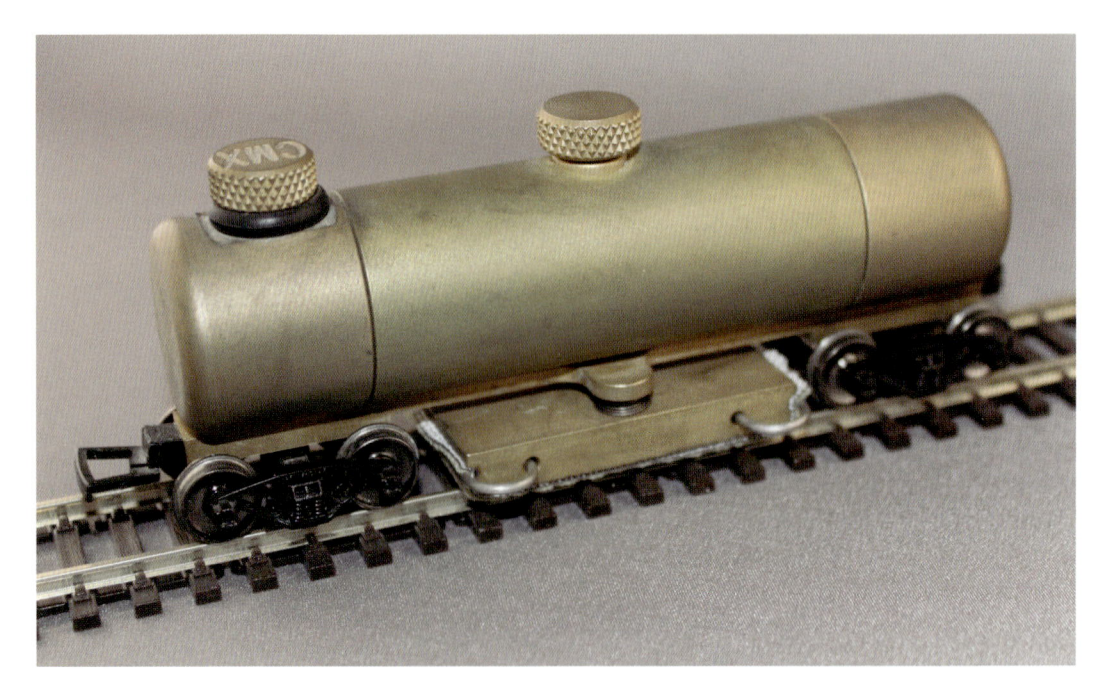

A rail-cleaning tanker wagon, as produced in several scales by CMX or in OO/HO by Sharge UK, filled with your choice of cleaning fluid and ideally pushed around in front of a large loco does an excellent maintenance rail-head clean before a running session. This is the author's CMX wagon. Dapol produces a multi-purpose rail and track cleaning car in OO/HO and the identical but smaller Tomix unit is available in N scale.

14
The '365' layout

I began to think of a new OO scale layout! My around-the-walls fixed layout – 'Elmswood' – had lost its appeal and was no longer being used. It was also fixed to three walls of one half of an integral double garage. I took the proverbial bull by the horns and began to dismantle the layout. I wanted to keep as much track as was possible, so it was necessary to remove as much of it undamaged as I could! All the scenic areas had been ballasted and stuck with diluted PVA glue. I applied almost boiling water in dribbles to the glued ballast on the points and managed to be able to soften and remove it, and save all but one point. The ballasted plain track I quickly decided to replace, as it was too much of an effort to try and de-glue that many lengths, but the non-scenic areas were carefully lifted and saved, as this area had not been ballasted. A box of 25 lengths of Peco SL-100 wooden-sleeper track was placed on order from my local model shop. Once all the track was lifted, all the scenic

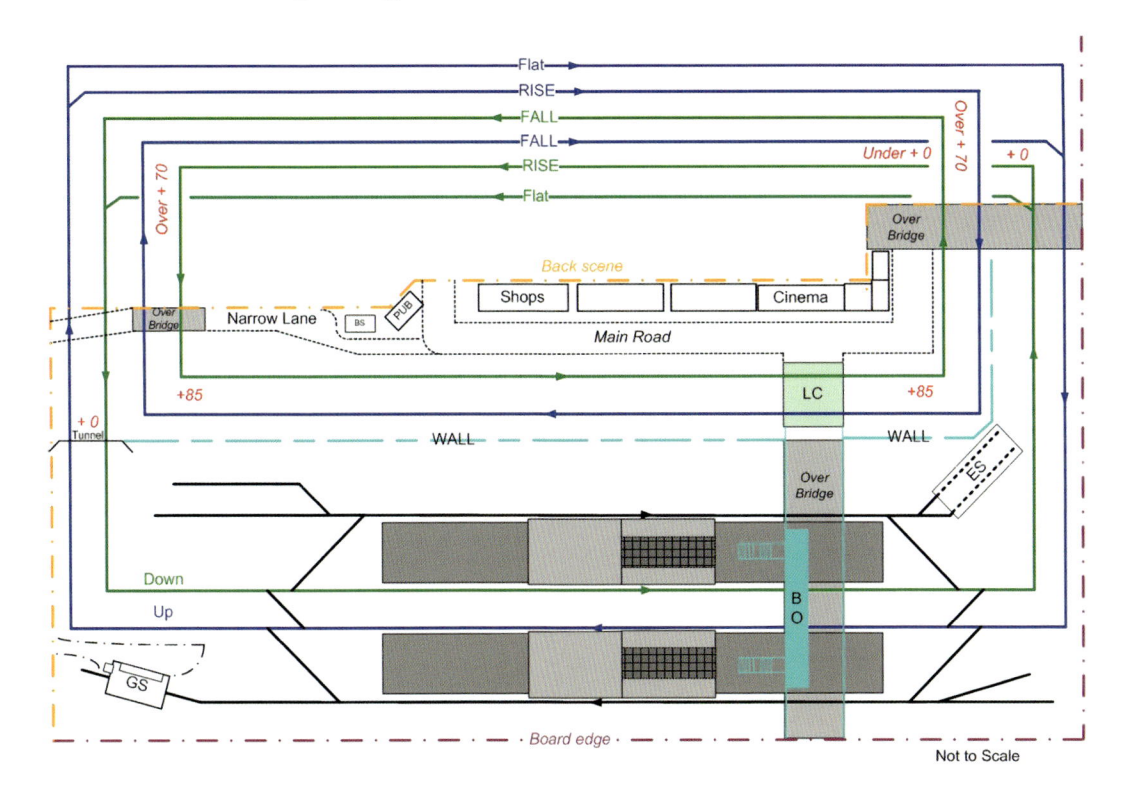

The proposed track plan for my 'High Hopes' layout. I would have liked the two pairs of crossover points to have been further out before and after the loop line points, but space and track curves restricted me!

items were removed, but many were not saved, as they were somewhat specific to that former layout. All the baseboards were cut up and most of the plywood and some timber taken to the council tip for disposal.

I must add a word of caution here regarding the removal of ballasted track or points. The use of boiling water is extremely dangerous, so only do this if you are 100% sure of what you are doing! Also, some water will inevitably seep through the baseboard holes and end up on the floor. In a garage this isn't too much of an issue, but if undertaken indoors I would highly recommend the laying of a sheet of plastic material under the layout to protect any flooring.

I now had a space of approximately 5.2 by 2.4 metres empty of a railway, to partly fill. But it was now full of plastic crates containing locos, rolling stock and track, etc. At the beginning of May I ordered online all the timber I considered I would need, and two full 2440 by 1220mm (8ft by 4ft) sheets of 11mm-thick OSB boarding for the baseboard tops (OSB is Oriented Strand Board, frequently used for shuttering-up work, especially where a building's windows have been damaged and a temporary cover is required). However, it is sold with a perfectly flat surface and is easily cut with a hand or power saw. It accepts and holds pins and screws well, and is far cheaper than plywood and safer to cut than MDF.

As this new layout was to be semi-portable and no longer fixed to the garage walls, I decided to use deeper outside framing with shallower internal bracing, so at the same time I ordered packs of 2.4-metre lengths of 69mm by 18mm and 21mm by 44mm PSE timber, boxes of wood screws in various lengths and a bottle of PVA woodworking glue. Unfortunately, something went very wrong with the order, although the money was taken! Following several telephone calls the whole order was eventually delivered on the last day of May!

The time spent waiting for the timber delivery was used to plan and refine the layout's track plan and produce a cutting list for the two 2440 by 1220mm boards, to avoid as much waste as possible. Points removed from the former layout were thoroughly cleaned of any still remaining ballast particles and given a general overhaul, and all their over-centre springs were removed; this was because I was going to be using servo motors to operate all of them.

On 1 June I began the build. It was Day 1 of the 365 days that I had allowed myself to construct a new layout and get it running, though not to fully complete it. Using the baseboard cutting list, the two sheets of OSB were marked for cutting and an electric circular saw used to make the cuts. The sheets sat on and were supported by two portable work benches. A hand panel saw could have been used, but the circular saw was quicker and a lot less effort!. Edges were sanded smooth, and

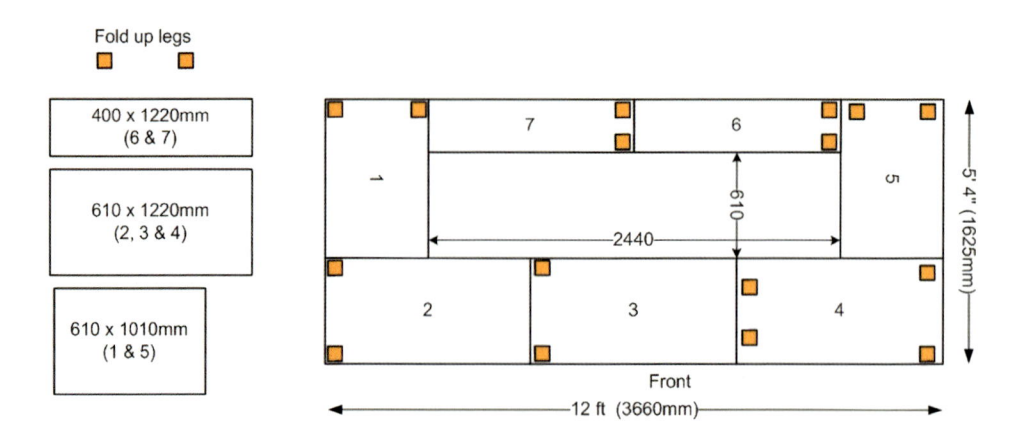

The basic baseboard configuration.

each cut section marked to correspond to the master cutting plan. In all, seven panels were cut from the two sheets: three were 1220 by 610mm, two 1010 by 610mm and two 1220 by 400mm. The two 400mm-wide boards were then duly cut into quarters lengthwise to produce four strips 100mm wide by 1220mm long. These would form two ramps and two flat baseboard tops.

A 210mm-wide strip was cut off the long edges of the two wider (front) boards, which was to be used for the higher level, and on the end corner boards the upper-level boards were cut at an angle to allow the curvature of the upper-level tracks at each end. As the layout was to be portable, I decided to make the

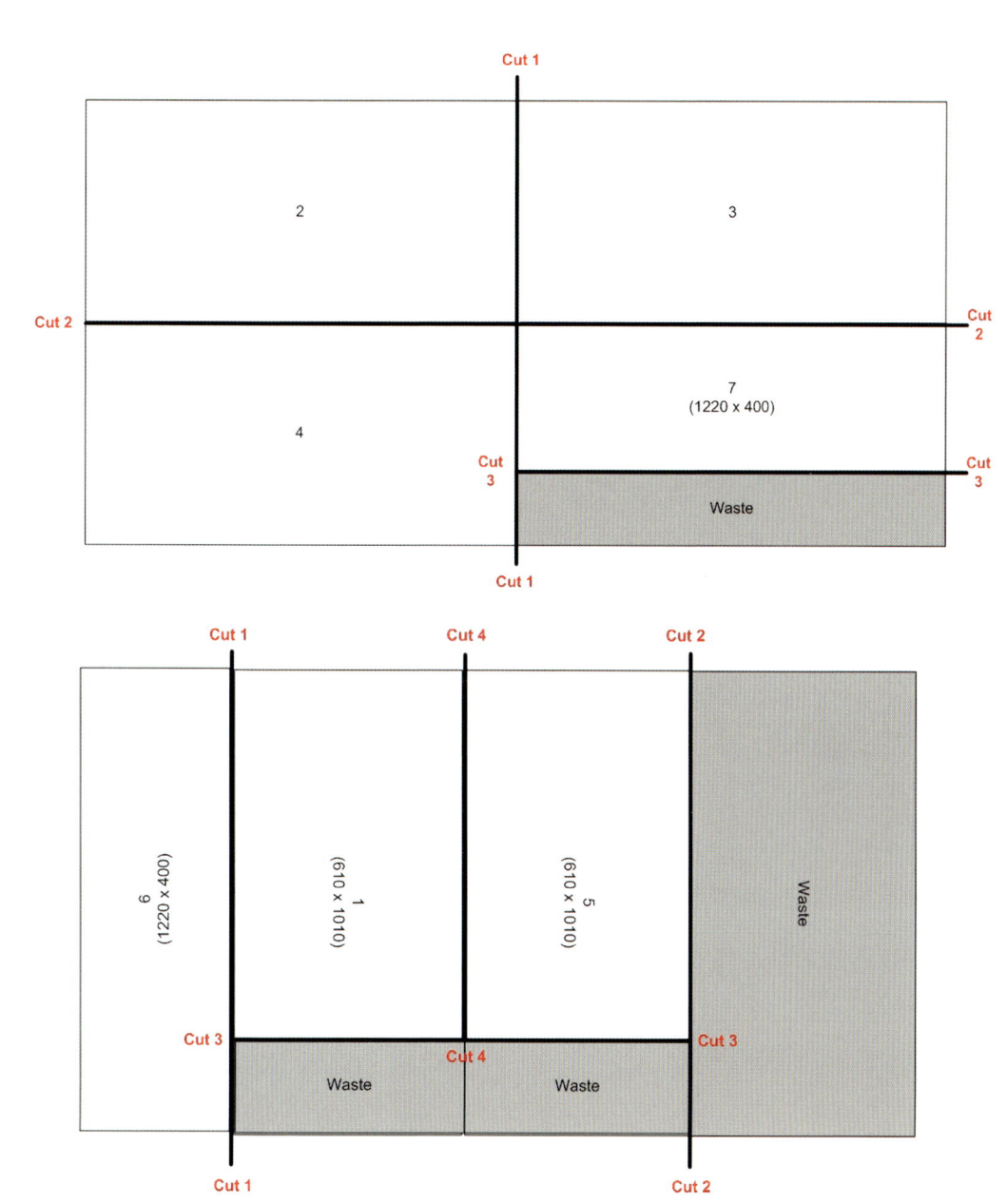

The cutting plan for the two OSB sheets.

supporting legs permanently attached, but able to be folded up inside the baseboard's deeper outer framing for transportation. 200mm-long tee-hinges are used to pivot each leg. Angled timber leg bracing was used to prevent the legs moving once lowered, and they were locked to the main baseboard framing and the legs' cross-bracing timber by using back-flap hinges that had their pivot pins removed and a split pin inserted to lock the brace in place at each end.

All the carpentry of the timbers (if you can really call it carpentry!) was undertaken using mainly an electric chop saw to provide a square cut. Square butt joints were used and all joints were PVA glued then secured together with suitable wood screws inserted into pre-drilled pilot holes to avoid the timber splitting. Once a basic frame had been produced, the baseboard top was PVA-glued and screwed to the timbers' narrow edges. Cross-bracing of shallower timber was cut to the required length to fit in between the deeper side frames, but before they were fitted they each had three 15mm-diameter holes drilled in their wider surface, close to the top edge; these were to allow wires to pass around the baseboard. Once prepared, the top edges and ends of the cross braces were coated in PVA glue and placed in the correct position;

The underside of the baseboard with the cross braces installed. Note the wiring access holes in the cross braces.

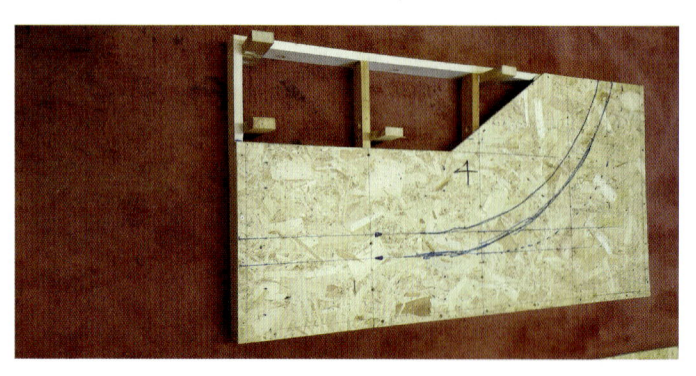

A section of the baseboard is cut away for use as the upper track level.

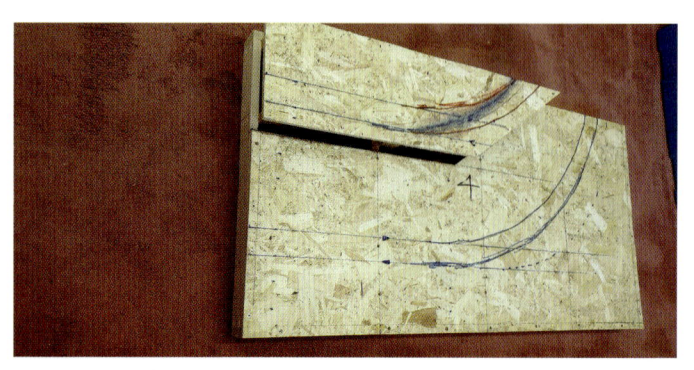

Now the upper-section board has been added and was cut to an angle to allow for the track curves. The drawn lines are just rough outlines of where the track will be positioned.

pilot holes were drilled in the side frames to allow woodscrews to pull up and securely clamp the cross braces in place. As soon as possible the boards were turned over and pilot holes drilled in the OSB surface along centre lines of the cross braces and screws inserted to pull up the cross braces to the OSB underside.

The accompanying photographs show the stages of baseboard construction, and how the framing and tops were assembled.

To prevent the legs from moving and folding up when the layout was erected, diagonal timber braces were fixed between the baseboard's cross-bracing timber and the legs' lower cross brace. These were removable when in transit, but were held in place by a simple pair of back-flap hinges top and bottom, with their pivot pins removed and replaced by a split pin. Adjustable feet were fitted to all legs to allow minor adjustments on uneven floors.

Once all the baseboards had been

The pivot pins are removed from the back-flap hinges and a split pin inserted. Each split pin is held to the layout or leg with a short length of chain to prevent it being lost.

The legs fold up within the baseboard's framing, and look like this when raised and ready for transportation.

constructed, pattern-maker's dowels (two per joint) were inserted into the end joints of the boards; these would ensure correct realignment of the boards when they were separated and joined back together again. Strong suitcase latches were fitted on each side of a pair of abutting boards to pull the boards tightly together. Then a coat of PVA diluted with water was applied to all surfaces to seal them.

Thoughts then turned to track-laying, drilling holes for point operation, etc, and connecting wiring from board to board. As DCC power was involved – which in my case can be up to around 4.0 amps – I opted to use 'aviation'-style four-pin plugs and sockets, 20mm diameter for DCC and 12-volt DC power around the layout, and 16mm diameter for the data pair of wires (more on this later) and a pair of spare wires.

Track-laying commenced with an initial decision on how to support the rail ends at the baseboard joints. I decided to use 1.6mm-thick copper-clad printed circuit board (PCB). An order for two sheets of board was placed and when they arrived they were cut into strips around 4-5mm wide using a slitting disc in an electric mini drill (Dremel). These PCB strips were then used as replacement sleepers at each board join where the tracks crossed. Initially they were drilled with a 0.8mm-diameter drill in two or three places depending on their length and glued in place with contact adhesive, then Peco track pins were inserted into the previously drilled holes to add to the secure fixing. A razor saw was used to carefully cut through the copper on each sleeper to remove any connection from rail to rail, and where a long strip was used to retain two tracks the copper was also cut between the tracks. The

Above: One of the diagonal timber leg braces in position.

The completed seven baseboards are seen connected together and sealed with a coat of PVA and water mixture.

Joining track across a baseboard join.

track was then laid in a continuous length and, once pinned in place, the rails were soldered on their outsides to the copper-clad sleepers. Once cooled, the rails were cut through with a razor saw used directly in line with the join of the two abutting boards.

Points were positioned and their drive pin holes marked on the baseboard surface. Each point was then removed and a pair of 4.5mm-diameter holes drilled side by side across the point's position. These holes were then opened up to make a 9mm by 4.5mm slot. As each point is an Electrofrog (live frog) type, holes were also drilled for the frog feed wire and two dropper wires connecting the outer stock rails to the DCC bus pair below. Each point had undergone full conversion when used on the previous layout: the two closure rails had their factory-installed gap link wires removed underneath, then the two dropper feed wires were stripped of their insulation by around 10mm and soldered to the underside of the outer stock rail and the underside of the adjacent closure rails. This allowed the moving switch blade rails to be at the same polarity as the adjacent stock rail and prevented two things: a) the possibility of metal wheels bridging a stock rail to the inner face of an open switch rail, which without the conversion would be at the opposing polarity, and b) the reliance on the switch rail on each side making 100% contact with the stock rails when closed, in order to pass power along the point. Once all the required wiring holes were drilled in the baseboard, the frog and two soldered on dropper wires were carefully passed down to beneath the baseboard for later connection. When I was fully satisfied, the point was correctly positioned and pinned down flat. Note that in all cases the Electrofrog points' frog wire was extended and thereby allowed connection to a change-over micro-switch operated by the servo's operating arm as it drove the point over.

Any gaps where sleepers were missing would have cosmetic sleepers glued to the baseboard. These are simply sleepers removed from a scrap piece of flexible track and their rail fixing chairs cut off; they can then be slid under the

Track-laying nears completion.

rail and positioned. Once glued in place and ballasted they appear to be exactly like rail-retaining sleepers. Prior to installation, each piece of track has two dropper wires soldered to the underside of the rails. These droppers pass down below the baseboard via a single 2mm-diameter hole drilled roughly central to the rails. Together with all the dropper wires on the points, they eventually connect to the larger DCC bus pair of wires.

As there are very many dropper wires under each board, and more in the station area, I opted to use a simple bus bar connection. The main DCC bus wire arrives and is connected into a four-way piece of terminal block. The mating outgoing bus wire connects into the next terminal along, and the same for the other bus wire, using position three and four of the terminal block. On the opposite side of the terminal block two short pieces of stripped copper wire are made into a sort of 'U' shape; one is inserted into blocks 1 and 2 and the other into blocks 3 and 4. This then allows the DCC to come in on 1 and 3 and leave via 2 and 4 terminals. The copper wires have several dropper wires soldered to them from the rails above. Numerous four-way blocks are fitted per board and many droppers soldered to each, keeping the overall length of each dropper to around a maximum of 300mm from rail to bus. I have used 32/0.2mm equipment wire for the bus pair in grey and orange colours, and the droppers are all 7/0.2mm wire in the same two insulation colours. When wiring the board's DCC droppers to the bus pair, I connect a battery-fed buzzer across the two main DCC bus wires and leave it connected while working. Should any dropper be accidently crossed over or a points' frog switch be wrongly wired, the buzzer immediately sounds and alerts you to the fact that there is a problem.

As previously mentioned, to connect all the electrics board-to-board I used 'aviation' connectors, as these offer a screw-on locking ring to retain the plug securely in place, and their current capacity exceeds anything I was likely to require. They do have one small problem in that their fixed socket, if mounted onto the front surface of the support framing timbers, extends beyond the front edge and makes it likely to be knocked or damaged during transportation of the layout. I decided to drill holes for each socket in the side frames and make them large enough to allow finger room for tightening and removal of the plugs. A hole of 32mm diameter was drilled for the 16mm socket, while a 45mm-diameter hole for

Typical terminal block and dropper connections.

Recessed socket holes on the side framing of the baseboard.

the 20mm socket. The sockets were mounted onto 6mm-thick ply, which was secured to the rear of the bracing timbers, thereby allowing the socket to be recessed and prevent any accidental damage occurring.

Point operation, point position indications plus detection of locos on the hidden storage lines are all carried out by MERG CBUS data units. MERG (Model Electronic Railway Group) is a producer and supplier of electronic kits for home assembly, and they can only be obtained if you are MERG member, which I am. I decided at an early stage to use CBUS as the main accessory operating method as it involves just two data wires and a regulated 12-volt DC power supply. The trains are controlled by DCC (Digital Command Control).

Over a period I purchased a number of MERG CBUS kits that allow servos to be operated or just provide outputs or accept inputs. These kits were made up and tested during periods when other items are awaited. Internet ordering has been a saviour; it does have a few issues regarding postage costs and occasionally delays in receiving ordered items, but in the main the sellers are very good and

A typical servo control board kit, made up and in work. This one operates just two servos, but has the capability to operate up to eight individual ones.

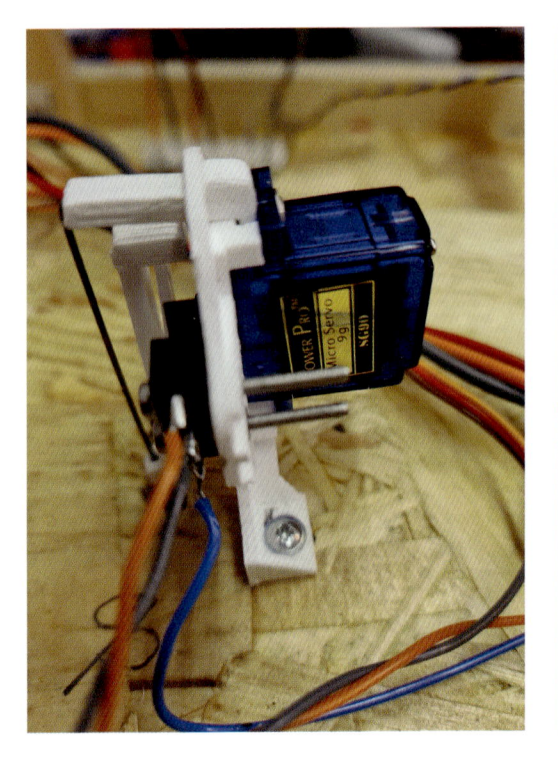

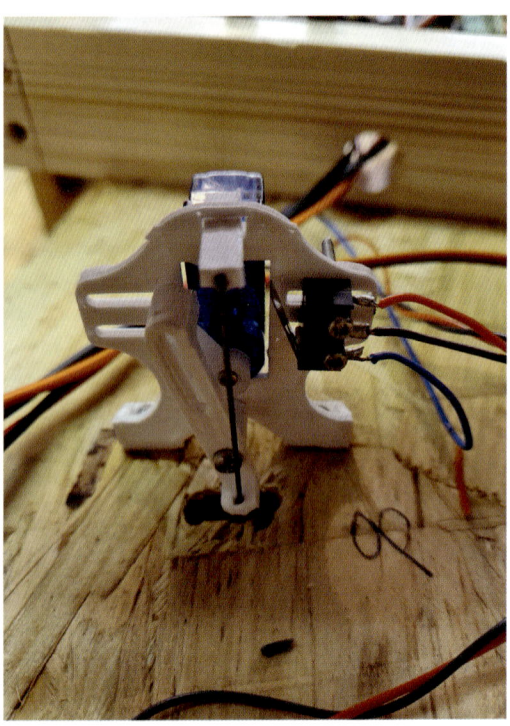

Side and front views of a servo operating a set of points. The servo's operating rod, which is made from flexible piano wire, holds the point over under light tension. Remember that all points have had their over-centre springs removed to allow slow movement of the point blades.

quick in supplying items ordered.

The great thing about servos is their relatively low cost and simplicity of operation. Once fitted to a specially produced servo mount, they can be adjusted for the amount of throw required left or right and the speed at which they move from one side to the other. This is all done via an electronic servo control board, and in my case a laptop computer gives the microchips the settings required. Once set, the laptop is no longer needed unless further adjustments are required. On the servo mount there are two positions to fix micro-switches, and I use one of these positions for frog polarity switching of the set of points being operated by the servo.

A control panel was designed and the panel's fascia produced on a PC using a drawing software package, at A3 size. The file was sent to a commercial printer, who printed the design onto an aluminium sheet. The sheet was then installed in a rectangular wooden frame, which had a groove cut all round to the thickness of the panel and some 5mm down from the top surface. All switches and LED holes were carefully drilled in the required places. (I did allow the drill bit to slip twice, but in the main everything went well!) I used 1.8mm 'tower'-style LEDs as these allow just their tops to appear on the panel's surface. Point operation was via a single-press non-locking push button for each set of points, or pair of points where a crossover pair were to move together. Point position LEDs were yellow to show which route had been set, and red LEDs lit up along the sections of track in the rear hidden sidings when a loco was present. A single blue LED showed that the CBUS data lines were working correctly. All this was operated by a MERG CBUS panel unit, capable of allowing up to 32 switches and 32 LEDs to be operated from the one board and over a twisted pair of wires from or to all boards on the layout. I use a 5-amp, 12-volt regulated power supply to feed

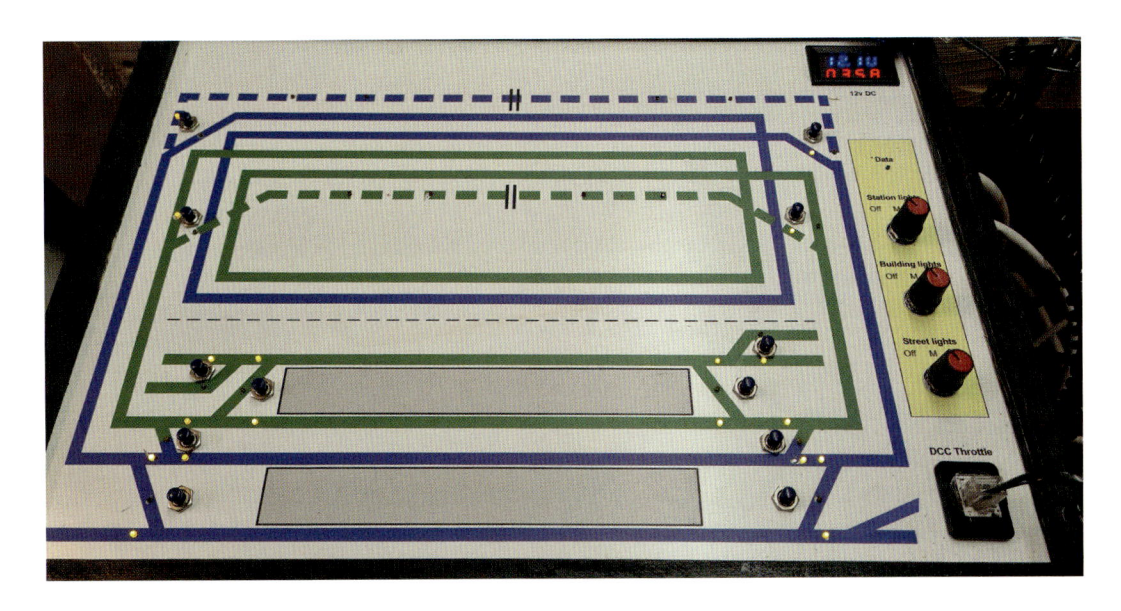

The control panel. The dotted lines on the control panel represent the up and down hidden storage lines, which can hold up to two trains per line. The sections are shown divided by two vertical lines, and each section has two red LEDs that illuminate when a loco occupies a section. On the right, top to bottom, are the 12-volt DC voltage and current power meter, three rotary switches for layout lighting controls, and at the bottom an RJ45 socket for the DCC handheld controller. The two grey rectangular sections along the bottom are the island platforms. The yellow LEDs show which route has been set by their respective sets of points; there are three LEDs on a pair of crossover points, and two LEDs on a single set of points.

all accessories and servos via their control boards; all the layout lights – buildings, street and platform lights – could be on at full power level or at a reduced level. The supply also powered all the panel LEDs via the panel unit. A DC voltage and current meter showed power levels on the 12-volt supply, and three three-position rotary switches provided the layout lighting selection of Low/Off/High brightness. The DCC Prodigy controller also had a socket in the panel, so all controls were self-contained within the one unit.

'Aviation' plugs and sockets provided feeds in and out of the panel and a 2.1mm DC barrel plug's socket allowed the 12 volts to be fed into the panel from an external power supply unit. A data USB input socket was also provided to allow a laptop to connect to the CBUS system when needed.

It became too cold in January to work in the garage even though it is integral to the main house. I could have used an electric heater, but that seemed too wasteful and needed to be turned on a long while before I ventured out there. So January and most of February were non-railway months! That wasted 50 or so of the 365 layout building days! But much time was spent indoors in the warm building construction kits or electronic items for the layout.

Late February was slightly milder and work resumed. All the electrics for track and CBUS modules were completed and by mid-March the moment of truth had come – it was switch-on time! I pushed the mains power socket switch and the servos sprang into life, moving to their required positions. Pressing push buttons on the panel allowed the appropriate servo(s) to drive over the points and the panel LEDs changed the route direction. Wonderful – it worked!

Next came the powering up of the DCC system. The power was applied and the handset lit, showing a normal display. Wow, that was working too! A DCC-fitted loco was placed on the rails and its address entered. Turning up the speed control knob saw the loco judder forward, then stop. Ah, a problem! In fact, it was only dirty rail tops, which in my eagerness to get things operational I had completely forgotten to clean. Out came the rail-cleaning fibre brush and about half an hour later every rail had been cleaned regardless of whether it was new or old. Back to the DCC controller and the same loco, the speed knob was once again turned up a little – not too fast in case any rail joints were incorrectly aligned, or other problems appeared. The loco ran very well, faltering on a couple of points which I discovered still had a tiny amount of ballast in their flangeways.

It also derailed where the transition between climb and level occurred on a curve on the upper level at the rear. Close inspection revealed that the rails where not quite aligned; one needed to be raised and moved slightly inwards. With the soldering iron heated and rail solder softened, the rail was repositioned with the aid of a pair of long-nosed pliers to hold it while it was resoldered. Once cooled, a finger run along the rail proved a smooth transition.

The loco was run around the layout and over the former problem joint, and all was good. Another loco was placed on the rails in the opposite direction and a couple of carriages added; some wagons were also added behind the first loco. Both were then set running, and all was good. Points were moved over to access the low-level rear storage lines and as each train passed over the rear section it illuminated the appropriate pair of red 'track section occupied' LEDs on the panel.

So, my '365-day' build had exceeded all my expectations. I still had all of April and May to undertake scenic work, but that was technically outside my self-imposed 365-day remit that I had allowed myself to construct the baseboards, wire everything and to get the new layout running. It could now offer running as frequently as required.

My first major scenic construction was an overbridge, which also carried the station entrance and booking office. It was constructed from 2mm-thick cardboard covered in Scalescene™ brick paper. In addition, I ordered four 15mm-deep 'I'-shaped plastic girders; these were painted a dark grey and three were

The overbridge in the early stages of construction, with the booking office building and stairs waiting to be fitted.

The station entrance at road level.

installed under the roadbed as supports. The booking office took some investigation, as the rear had to have a footbridge walkway attached to it to allow passengers to descend to the two island platforms; to add to the problem, the bridge and booking office were on the edge of one baseboard while the stairs and walkway were on the abutting board! I eventually found a suitable station building kit produced by LCUT™ in the form of a laser-cut building, which was turned through 180 degrees to make the original platform canopy side the station building entrance and the former flat side the rear. Windows in the rear side were covered over on the inside of the building, and a footbridge from the Scalescene range was printed and constructed in card with alterations to the walkway roof and the addition of an 'I' girder under the walkway. Once installed, the footbridge abutted tightly to the rear of the booking office and allowed passengers access to and from the platforms below.

The two island platforms were to be around 1.5 metres long and were made using plastic cable trunking as the base, which is 15mm tall and 25mm wide. A 2mm cardboard surface was glued on top once brick paper had been glued to the sides of the trunking. Once all was dry, Scalescene platform surface paper was printed and carefully glued to the card. The reason I used cable trunking as a base foundation for the platforms was twofold: I already had several lengths in my loft, and it was far cheaper than obtaining 15mm timber and much quicker than making the base from 15mm-deep strips of cardboard.

Two island platform buildings were needed, and one was constructed from a Scalescene design to test its appearance – it looked good in my opinion. A second was then produced.

Above: The footbridge waiting to be added to the platforms; it will abut to the rear wall of the booking office.

Right: The footbridge in place against the rear of the booking office building.

was the answer and I chose to use a gated crossing rather than barriers, as gates were more in keeping with my modelling era (1950s to 1960s). A suitable kit was procured and using Wills timber decking plastic card I constructed a road and pedestrian crossing that abutted the overbridge roadway.

A backscene of 6mm-thick MDF was cut to a height of approximately 300mm/12 inches and given two coats of sky-blue matt emulsion paint. Once dried, the backscene were fixed to the rear of the layout with the aid of 30mm-long M6 bolts, large washers and M6 tee nuts fitted into the insides of the layout's wooden frame. A selection of low-relief buildings were ordered and constructed, with some shops and offices having LED lighting installed. The main road surface was made from sheets of printed 'tarmac' road surface produced on an inkjet printer on A3 paper, and laid onto 2mm-thick card, which was cut to the road size. Onto this was placed a 1mm-thick card pavement and kerb fixed down before the buildings were stuck into place, but only after small holes had been drilled for the building lighting wires to pass down to below the baseboard.

Platform construction: note the cable trunking used as a base.

I needed a means of road access from the overbridge to the rear of the upper level so that road traffic and people could safely cross the two main lines on the upper level where shops and houses were to be installed. A level crossing

As a scenic break, a long road bridge was constructed to run the full depth of the baseboard; together with the blue-painted backboards it provided the natural break to the rear tracks, which were not viewable.

A rear wall was required to cover the gap between the lower and upper levels behind the station area. I constructed a 1.2-metre-long arched retaining wall for the main area, seen here with the first of the two island platform buildings.

The long road overbridge takes shape. It was made from card uprights covered in brick-effect paper and Peco girder bridge sides painted dark grey.

On the lower board level to the left of the bridge I introduced a Signal & Telegraph (S&T) depot. The base for this was again 2mm-thick card covered with an inkjet-printed sheet of block brick effect paper. A main office building was added and a lean-to covered storage area. Cable drums, oil drums, concrete cable troughing, staff and other small items were added to the scene to enhance the overall appearance and to add realism.

Left: The road bridge finished, with vehicles already using it!

Below: The road is 2mm-thick card covered in printed 'tarmac' paper. A path was added, running down the left-hand side.

Right: The base for the S&T depot has been glued in place and a fence fixed around its perimeter.

Above: The card base of the depot raises the area just above baseboard level. Several detailing items have been added, but the surrounding area still has to be fully detailed.

Top left: The track passing the depot has been ballasted.

Fencing has been added to the upper level, together with the main road, which passes under the bridge. A zebra crossing with two working Belisha beacon lamps has been fitted and wired up to a 12-volt DC power supply. The Co-op corner store was built from a full-size card kit, which was cut in half depth-wise to allow it to become a low-relief corner building; it is sitting on the right-angle corner of the backscene.

Attention was now turned to the front right-hand corner of the layout. This was to become a Permanent Way depot, with a short piece of track leading into it. A 2mm-thick card base was covered this time in cobblestone-effect printed paper and a slot cut for the track, which was level with the top surface of the board. This meant that the whole area was raised slightly on more 2mm cardboard to bring the final surface up to rail level.

Left and above right: Fixing the base for the Permanent Way depot.

A wooden fence was fixed around the perimeter and two ready-made buildings added. A pile of sleepers, rails, point stock and switches and other detailing parts were all glued to the area. A Wickham motorised trolley was purchased, which sat on the rails inside the depot. The new 'Civil Engineers' Morris Traveller car was parked next to the main workshops, and a BR Land-Rover was waiting to enter once the gate was opened. Working yard lighting was installed and the whole yard area given a dirty look by air-brushing with very diluted black acrylic paint over most of the cobbles.

The Permanent Way depot takes shape, with basic detailing added.

The Permanent Way depot with track inlaid in the cobbles.

The 'Moggie' – Morris Minor Traveller – and a Wickham trolley in place.

The High Hopes helicopter has been out and snapped an aerial view of the P Way depot!

A signal box and engine shed were positioned, and scenic scatters added around them. The tracks leading up to the station platform ramps was fully ballasted, great care being taken to ensure that no ballast or its fixing diluted PVA glue was able to get into the points' check rails and frog areas, the gap in the switch rails or the opening for the drive pin.

On the upper level, a town High Street scene was created. Road and pavements were installed using the now 'standard' 2mm and 1mm thick cardboard faced with printed papers.

The signal box and engine shed area before and after detailing.

Above and below: The tracks leading up to the level crossing on the high level before and after ballasting. Scatters have been added between the track and the retaining wall and roadside fence.

With the lights turned on the scene comes to life!

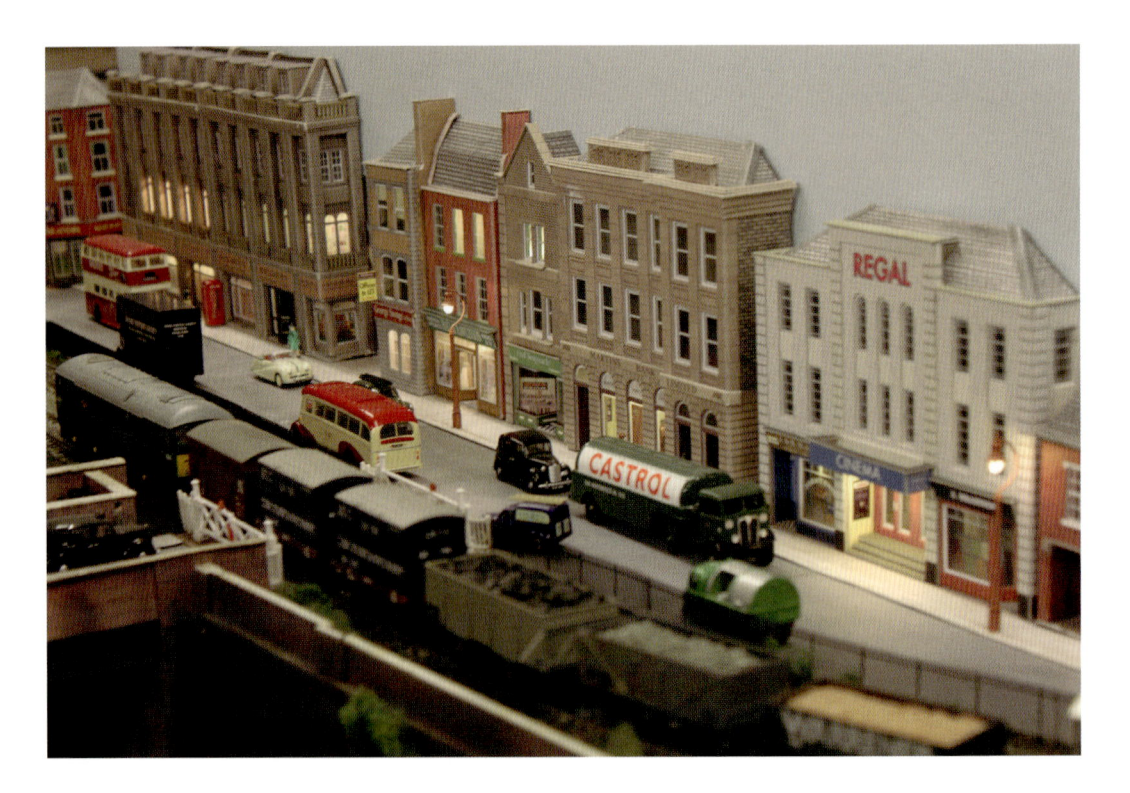

Dusk falls over High Hopes and the building and street lights are turned on.

All the buildings were low-relief kits and had LED lighting fitted into various sections – but not all rooms were lit.

The next item to work on was installing street lighting. I acquired nine LED streetlights from a model railway lighting supplier and these needed suitable holes to be drilled through the pavements and into the baseboard. The fine wires for the lights were passed down to below the baseboard and a Series 1K (1000-ohm) resistor added to each light. Then each lamp was connected to the 'street lighting supply', which was adjustable in voltage to dim all the lamps as required.

Signalling was in the form of three-aspect colour-light signals, and three were initially fitted and wired. One had a junction indicator on top of its main signal head and the other two were in the station on the up line, one on a wall mount and the other fixed onto the girder of the station overbridge. They were all operated by electronic signalling control units and infra-red train detectors produced from self-assembly kits supplied by MERG (Model Electronic Railway Group).

The platform tracks were then ballasted, as well as and the tracks in front of the High Street on the upper level. Fencing was installed

The Down Home signal with a junction indicator ('feather') can just be glimpsed above the breakdown crane. The 'feather' is lit as the road is set to the down platform loop.

An up express thunders through the station on green signals, while a 'Deltic' waits in the up loop for the tracks to become clear. A freight train trundles over the level crossing on the upper level.

between upper tracks and the High Street, and scenic scatters added to enhance the cess area between ballast and fence line.

The station canopies were extended by one full length on each platform and held on supporting columns produced from two sizes of plastic tubing – approximately 4mm and 6.5mm in diameter. The upper section of each column fitted tightly inside the wider lower section, which was in turn fitted into drilled holes in the platform surface; the smaller upper section column fitted into drilled holes in the underside of the new canopies. This allowed adjustment of the height of the canopy before each column was glued into place.

Two LED strips of three warm white LEDs per strip were added before the canopies were fitted in place, and two strips were fitted on each side of each canopy (four strips per canopy in all). Their feed wires, made of very thin Kynar wire, were soldered onto each strip, then run down the inside of one of the canopy support columns; the hole for the larger tube section was extended through the baseboard to allow the wires to pass to the underside, then onto the wiring connections for the 12-volt lighting feeds. The columns were painted in a maroon colour.

Two newspaper kiosks, made from Dapol kits, were added, one on each platform. A Ratio modular covered footbridge kit was obtained, which would fit just after the ends of the new canopies to allow passengers to cross between platforms. Being modular, the width of the footbridge between staircases could be adjusted during building so as to fit as near as possible to the platform centre lines.

At the far left-hand end of the layout there was to be a tunnel for the lower-level tracks to access the off-scene rear loops, and a bridge over the upper-level tracks, which again led to the off-scene loops. First I trialled a ready-made tunnel portal, but found it to be too narrow; the carriages were hitting the tunnel sides on the curved tracks. I therefore made a double-track tunnel portal from a Scalescenes download in card and printed paper. The width of the portal allowed it to be positioned on a curved double track, and the longest carriages cleared the portal sides easily. Once the portal was positioned and glued in place, a brick-effect lining about 100mm long was glued to the inside of the portal to represent the inside of the tunnel. I then constructed the last of the long retaining walls, taking the wall from the station area round to the tunnel.

To make the embankments, card strips were produced as lattice formers and supports on each side of the tunnel. The strips were cut approximately 10mm wide and fixed in place with hot melt glue. Once the latticework was complete the area was covered in two layers of plaster bandage; the tracks below, and the tunnel side wall, were covered in 50mm-wide masking tape to prevent contamination from the wet plaster bandage during application. After some 48 hours the plaster bandage had set rock hard and was then painted with a coat of artist's Burnt Umber acrylic, which gave a reasonably good representation of brown earth colour. Once the paint was dry the area was coated in neat PVA adhesive and static grass applied via a static grass applicator tool. Additional bushes and course ground cover were placed in the area, created using various scenic materials from mainly Woodland Scenics. All were glued in place with neat PVA. Three trees were 'planted' on the embankment slopes.

The area above the tunnel was to represent a narrow country lane, leading from a road junction on the main High Street near the pub, up a slope, onto a plate girder bridge over the tracks, then off scene at the extreme left-hand side. The rear edge of the road had a hedgerow against the backscene boards, and at the lower end a bus shelter was added. All road surfaces were inkjet printed at home onto A3 sheets from Scalescenes downloads and cut to size to suit the section of roadway.

All the printed surfaces – roadways, walls, tunnel portal, etc – were then given two coats of spray matt varnish to protect them.

Two sidings were laid, stopping short of the tunnel, and were to be used for storage of

The platform canopy supports and newspaper kiosks.

locos or diesel multiple units. A suitable small building was used to represent the loco crew messroom and booking-on office. A permanent way hut was located near the tunnel entrance to serve the local permanent way gang who look after the track in the tunnel and its approaches.

A new signal box and goods shed were obtained for the left-hand end, then full scenic detailing could commence in the area.

The following series of pictures shows the area during construction.

The twin platform signals, shown in the final picture of the sequence, were wired to a dual infrared train detector (MERG Hector kits) and a simple home-made dual electronic timer. One infrared detector was located in the crossover track from the loop line to the main line and the other just off the platform ramp end in the main line. These automatically control the aspects of the signal, as too does the position of the crossover points. Once the infrared detector has been activated by a passing train the appropriate signal reverts to a red aspect; an electronic PIC timer allows the signal to remain at red for some 7 seconds, even though the infrared detector has cleared following the passing of the train. After 7 seconds the PIC turns off the red aspect and allows the yellow aspect to be displayed for a further 7 seconds, then the aspect returns to green. This sequence applies to both signalled routes. The total of 14 seconds from red to green should allow ample time for a train to disappear fully into the rear off-scene area. However, should the tail end of a carriage or goods train still remain visible, the 7-second timer can easily be increased to a longer time

The first picture shows the beginnings of the country lane leading up to the overbridge from the High Street. The two lower sidings were later altered to make them a little longer by moving their entrance point nearer the station and laying the track straight rather than slightly offset to the right as shown here.

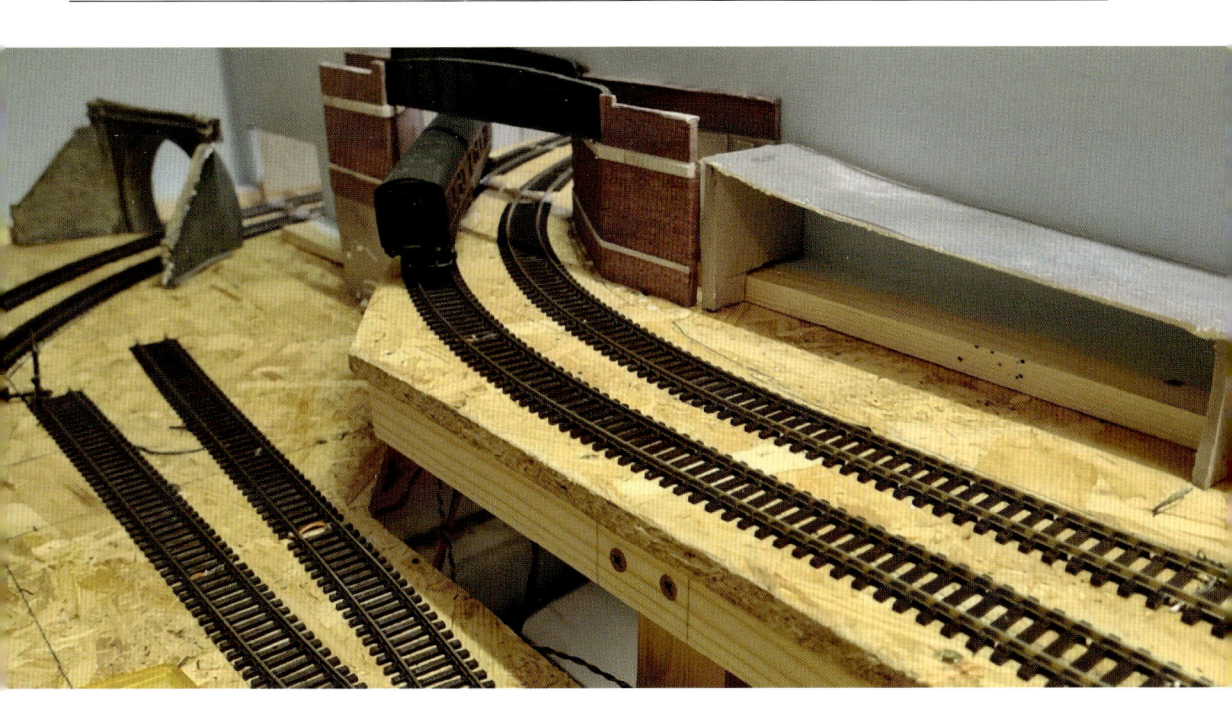

The earlier ready-made tunnel portal was subsequently replaced by a Scalescenes home-printed version. Once temporarily installed, it was tested using different carriages on both lines to ensure that none would touch the tunnel sides.

The final tunnel portal is glued in place and the card latticework has been glued all around to make the frame for the embankment. A retaining wall has been added to the section between the lower and upper levels.

The embankments have been covered in two layers of plaster bandage and the track protection masking tape has been removed.

The area has been scenically treated and trees added, and a fence separates the lane from the embankment. The next task is to ballast all the tracks.

The retaining wall for the lane was produced from more Scalescenes downloadable prints; once printed and allowed to dry, the paper was glued to a cardboard former produced to the desired wall height, which in this case is gradually increasing to follow the rise of the roadway, plus about a further 18mm to act as the parapet wall. The upper-level tracks have now been ballasted and ground cover added to both sides. A hedgerow borders the rear of the roadway and two gates have been installed to allow access to the fields beyond the hedge. A photographic back scene will be added later to represent fields stretching into the distance.

The pub is partly lit and the lane area is all but scenically completed. I felt that the backboard here could do with an image of a road leading away from the main road after its 90-degree turn, but to date I haven't found anything suitable. Unfortunately I'm no artist, so a hand-painted scene was not on the cards!

delay before a yellow aspect is permitted to be displayed.

It is now 31 May and 365 days have passed. I have a fully working layout with all electrics installed and tested, points all power-operated by servo motors from the control panel, trains running and around 80% of the scenic work completed. I never intended to fully complete the detailing in the one year allowed; in fact, a model railway is usually never completed, as frequently there are things to add or move, etc. But I reached my goal with ample time to spare. In fact, had I worked on the layout for the full 365 days the left-hand end would have been scenically all but completed! But the cold winter months in the garage didn't help, together with delays in receiving items needed due to everything requiring to be ordered online and delivered. But those are my excuses and I'm sticking to them!

I hope you have found this '365' build of interest and helpful in gaining some inspiration on how I'm building a medium-sized OO-scale layout. Ongoing work on this layout can also be viewed on my website under the 'High Hopes' heading.

A general view of the area, with detailing still to be done. The tracks are to be ballasted, the goods shed blended in and a yard area to be created around it. The narrow signal box fits nicely between main line and sidings and will be eventually be lit and internally detailed. A couple or three LED-lit yard lamps will be fitted along the retaining wall on the lower level, as this will be a walkway from the station to the small depot at the end of the sidings.